MIDRASH:

"COMPETITION AMONG THE NATIONS"

On page 180, you will discover why Jesus was a **religious pluralist**. When a scholar summarized the essence of religion as love of God and love of neighbor, Jesus embraced him warmly, saying, "You are not far from the kingdom of God." Notice that Jesus did not ask this man to accept him as his "personal Lord and Savior." He did not insist on doctrine. He did not seek to found a new religion or to exclude anyone. He simply said, "Love God and love your neighbor."

Jesus would never have called the Prophet Muhammad a "terrorist," as one of America's most prominent Christian preachers did on 60 Minutes. Nor would Jesus have called Islam an "evil and wicked religion," as another prominent preacher did. The Qur'an says, "If God had willed it, he could have made you a single nation. But he wanted to create competition among the nations, to see who would win the

prize for good deeds

(Sura 5.48). We should indeed compete with one another, says Allah, but not to kill or to conquer, but to do good deeds. And those who do the most good deeds, win. Can there be a more urgent competition than this?

THE
LOST
SPIRITUAL
WORLD™

The Scholars Version

Translation Panel

Editor in Chief

Robert W. Funk
Westar Institute

General Editors

Daryl D. Schmidt
Texas Christian University

Julian V. Hills
Marquette University

Editors, Apocryphal Gospels

Ron Cameron
Wesleyan University

Karen L. King
Occidental College

Translation Panel

Harold Attridge
University of Notre Dame

Helmut Koester
Harvard University

Edward F. Beutner
Westar Institute

Lane C. McGaughty
Williamette University

J. Dominic Crossan
DePaul University

Marvin W. Meyer
Chapman College

Jon B. Daniels
Defiance College

Robert J. Miller
Midway College

Arthur J. Dewey
Xavier University

Stephen J. Patterson
Eden Theological Seminary

Robert T. Fortna
Vassar College

Bernard Brandon Scott
Phillips Graduate Seminar

Ronald F. Hock
University of Souther California

Philip Sellew
University of Minnesota

Roy W. Hoover
Whitman College

Chris Shea
Ball State University

Arland D. Jacobson
Concordia College

Mahlon H. Smith
Rutgers University

Note: The above panel members were involved in the translation only. The artwork and commentary in this book were created separately. No involvement or endorsement by the panel is implied or suggested.

THE
LOST
SPIRITUAL
WORLD™

Unabridged translation of the Gospel of Mark

THE SCHOLARS VERSION

Select illustrations by

ALEJANDRA VERNON

Commentary, computer art & design by

RUTH RIMM

The Global Renaissance Society

New York

With love, dedicated to:

John Assaraf
Ian Clayton
The Dalai Lama
Wayne Dyer
Jane Fonda
Richard Gere
Jim Hardt
Yahya Hendi
Kelly Howell
Arianna Huffington
Vic Johnson
Horst & Inge Köhler
Rabbi Michael Lerner
Benoit Mandelbrot
Curt Matthews
Bill Moyers
Tony Robbins
Howard Schultz
Murray Smith
Eric Wood

"The crisis that the world finds itself in as it swings on the hinge of a new millennium is located in something deeper than particular ways of organizing political systems and economies. In different ways, the East and West are going through a single common crisis whose cause is the **spiritual** condition of the modern world. That condition is characterized by **loss**—the loss of religious certainties and of transcendence with its larger horizons.

Huston Smith
Why Religion Matters

CONTENTS

FURTHER READING

Introduction

Imagine sitting on the edge of a boat with all of your scuba gear on, lost and lonely, shivering in a deep spiritual freeze. If you take the plunge, will you find God? Or will you be heartbroken once again? Or drown? Or get eaten by the sharks?

Your third millennium beliefs warn you not to take the plunge. After all, you live in an astonishing age of Science. Even the great Danish philosopher Søren Kierkegaard said — over a century ago — that the Gospel stories are "absurd." But Kierkegaard was not mocking. He was despairing. He was acknowledging that given the progress of science and reason, Christianity was no longer believable.

I, too, am hovering on the edge of disbelief. I am like the one who cried in Mark 9:24, "Help my unbelief!" These are three of the most heartbreaking words in the Bible. A father is trying to heal his son, and he cannot for the moment, because he cannot believe. He believes that the sun revolves around the earth. He believes in supernatural demons and evil spirits. He believes that the earth is flat. He believes in all of these crazy things, but here he is, crying his heart out to a man named Jesus, because he still suffers from disbelief.

Here was a man of first century Galilee who was having just as much trouble believing in Jesus as you and I are. If it was difficult in a pre-scientific era for this man to believe in a "son of God" with supposedly supernatural powers, imagine how difficult it is for us — enlightened spiritual seekers of the third millennium — to believe in Jesus. "Help my unbelief" is the quintessential expression of our postmodern predicament.

Modern Science has thrust many of us into a vortex of despair. We are wired with spiritual needs, wired to seek a God in whom many of us can no longer believe. So here we are, in the boat, with our scuba gear on, ready to dive in, yet sadly unable to dive in. The strangest thing about this 21st century American funk is that one would think — based on numerous public opinion polls — that the Enlightenment never took place, that writers such as Emerson, Kierkegaard, Nietzsche and Spong never existed, and that miracles, supernatural healings, virgin births and bodily resurrections are all reasonable to believe. It's as if we're living in a spiritual time warp, swirling in the absurdity of trying to find a second millennium God in a third millennium world.

The Parable of the Scuba Diver

If you look toward the shore, you can see others in the water — some to their toes, others to their knees, others to their necks. But something stirs you to be more than just a dabbler. You may have probed the waters of religion before but walked away with an aching thirst. You are too honest with yourself: these ancient wisdom traditions often seem just as outdated as the belief that the sun revolves around the earth.

So this is it — what Matthew Arnold in his haunting poem, *Dover Beach*, described as the "melancholy, long, withdrawing roar" of "the Sea of Faith," where there is "neither joy, nor love, nor light, nor certitude, nor peace, nor help for pain." You must find a new light, a new peace, a new way of understanding the old faiths. But how?

The great psychologist Carl Jung, himself a nonbeliever, said, "No matter what the world thinks about religious experience, the one who has it possesses a great treasure. It provides him with a source of life, meaning and beauty, and gives a new splendor to the world and to mankind." To never fully immerse yourself in this great treasure, to live your life on a boat as a mere observer: this is tragic. And to die on the boat, knowing life only from the surface when there might be a lost ocean of indescribable beauty waiting to be discovered: this is even more tragic.

The Buddha warned his followers not to accept his teachings on blind faith but to put them to the test in their own lives, to experience Buddhism not as an intellectual exercise but in the deepest chambers of the heart. You ruin your capacity to experience God if you insist on "the facts, nothing but facts," as a character of Dickens once said. If you worry whether or not the stories in the Bible are factually true, then you become enslaved to the facts, enslaved to a materialist, reductionist form of spirituality. The facts are on the boat. You leave the facts behind when you dive into God's Sea.

In these pages, you will discover a way to suspend your skepticism and disbelief and open your heart to a trove of lost spiritual treasures. The one thing Jesus, the Buddha, Lao Tzu, Muhammad and the other great prophets seem to agree on is this: you cannot reason your way to God in any kind of black and white, linear way. You have to dive in. You have to make the leap.

Deep beneath the surface,

there are no more arguments, no more denominations, no more doctrines, no more requirements to believe. This Sea is known by a single word: **love**.

Now you can welcome the despair of which Kierkegaard wrote, for the despair breaks your heart and with your heart broken you find **love**; in **love** you find God.

Now you can marvel at all of God's beautiful and exotic creations. Imagine: from the dust of stars came this! That you are alive is a **miracle** beyond belief. A pit stop in paradise, this life. As Whitman said,

Seeing and hearing and feeling are **miracles**,
and each part and tag of me is a **miracle**.

Every hour of the light and dark is a **miracle**.
Every inch of space is a **miracle**.

That God has put this book into your hands is a **miracle**, too. Because no matter how skeptical you are, no matter how much you doubt the literal truth of our wisdom traditions, buried deep inside of you is a loving heart. Love is God's vitamin C, his cure for the most common cold of all —a cold heart.

"A BROKEN HEART OPENS THE GATES TO THE DIVINE PALACE."

THE BAAL SHEM-TOV

LOVE

love love love love love
love love love love love
love love love love love

love love love love love
love love love love love
love love love love love

love love love love love
love love love love love
love love love love love

"YOU DON'T HAVE TO BELIEVE IN GOD
IN ORDER TO EXPERIENCE GOD."

DEEPAK CHOPRA

There are those who say, "Only from our boat can you dive into God's Sea." How silly! Maybe the Christian boat has a nicer deck, maybe the Hindu boat has better diving equipment, maybe the Jewish boat has the best view, but the Sea is the Sea, and anyone can jump in. God cares little from which boat. I know because somehow, miraculously, I found God when I jumped from the boat of Unbelief.

The boat of Unbelief is just as good a launching pad as any other. You find God the moment you let go of the need to believe. God is neither a belief nor a set of doctrines; God is a **leap**, an **encounter**, an **experience** of an unfathomably rich spiritual Sea.

There is a boat for every faith and every denomination —whether Protestant or Catholic, Sunni or Shiite, Orthodox Jewish or Reformed. You can dive into God's Sea of love from any boat. Boats may come and go, but

the loving heart beats on.

heart beats

heart beats

heart beats

heart beats

heart beats

The great wisdom traditions give birth to the mystical sense within you. Through poetry and metaphor, they deepen your awareness of a Cosmic Creative Energy far greater than your own. But if this Energy we call God is infinite, then no man-made religion can ever fully encompass it.

Jesus never said: argue among yourselves about the factual truth or untruth of the Bible. He never preoccupied himself with what we third millennium readers regard as "historical truth." And the Gospel writers never said, "Jesus literally healed" or "Jesus metaphorically healed." They simply said, "Jesus healed." Literal or metaphorical: who cares? The question is: **how can we be healed?**

In these pages, you will discover a way to extract the spiritual nectar of our wisdom traditions without having to believe in any of the religious doctrines. You will find that this Energy Source called God has the power to rinse away your sorrows, to

Shampoo you in love

and to flood you with forgiveness.

Despite my lifelong yearning to connect with God, I could not believe in the Bible. Then when I read that verse in Mark 9:24, I found an almost **magical opening**, an astonishing way of connecting to God. My great epiphany was that I was looking for God in the boat. I was thinking of God as a Deity with a capital D, a supernatural force "out there" who caters to my needs on the surface. Instead I discovered that God is the key to the human heart. This is what John and Paul meant when they said,

God is love.

"In my father's house are many mansions," said Jesus (John 14:1). There is a **Buddhist** mansion, a **Hindu** mansion, a **Muslim** mansion, a **Jewish** mansion, a **Taoist** mansion, a **Jainist** mansion, a **Sikh** mansion, a **Shinto** mansion, a **Zoroastrian** mansion, a **Native American** mansion, a **Wicca** mansion, a **Gaia** mansion, a **Skeptic's** mansion, a **Christian** mansion—a mansion for people of all faiths and people of no faiths.

God says: you have a

Mansion for a Heart,

a kingdom for a soul,
just waiting to be born.

"THE GOAL OF ALL RELIGIONS IS THE SAME,
BUT THE LANGUAGE OF THE TEACHERS DIFFERS."

SWAMI VIVEKANANDA

The Teachings of Silvanus, one of the early writings of the
Alexandrian Christians discovered at Nag Hammadi, states
simply, "Accept Christ as **a good teacher**" (90:33-91:1).
Indeed, you may prefer to call Jesus "a good teacher."
There is a boat for you, too, as Jesus explicitly respected
this viewpoint—even in the canonical texts. In Mark 12:34,
when a Jewish scholar says that the two great commandments are to love God and love your neighbor, Jesus says of
him, "You are not far from the kingdom of God." According
to Jesus himself, you need not accept him as your "personal
Lord and Savior" and need not believe in any of the doctrines to partake of the kingdom of God.

Jesus never said,
"Believe in God and believe in your neighbor."

Jesus said,
"Love God and love your neighbor."

That is why, on page 182 of this book, you will see Jesus
warmly embracing a Pharisee (or what today we might call
an Orthodox Jew.) In our fractured world, Mark 12:34 is
arguably the single most important verse of Scripture.

Interfaith dialogue
is the only way our
world will survive into the next century.

Jesus never required that your beliefs violate the laws of Science. No believer has ever literally moved a mountain or walked on the sea. His deeper teachings show that your mountains and seas are mostly spiritual, mostly self-induced limitations of the mind. Jesus is the archetype of a great **Liberator** and **Transformer**, teaching you how to free yourself from the shackles of your mind. If there is any truth to the Satan metaphor, it is in your fears, doubts, worries and anxieties.

Consider why Rick Warren's doctrinally conservative best-seller, The Purpose Driven Life, was able to stop a murder. When Ashley Smith was abducted, she told the murderer about this remarkable **Energy Source** that Jesus tapped into. She did not first espouse a laundry list of archaic doctrines: the virgin birth, the trinity or the resurrection. They did not debate evolution or quantum physics. Ashley was never even on the boat that day—she ministered to the murderer from the depths of God's Sea. The Cosmic Christ has this power to transform a life—and this power is independent of dogma or doctrine.

You can still believe in Science and find deep spiritual rewards in exploring our wisdom traditions. That

We evolved from apes

or that the universe is billions of years old only deepens the mystery. The magic of our wisdom traditions is that in a highly evolved, technological culture, they can still show you how to experience the sacred. They can still show you **how to leap** into spiritual dimensions that not even our best scientists can comprehend.

There are those within the Church who, upon learning that your beliefs are different from theirs, do not respectfully say, "My beliefs are different from yours. But that's OK, we're all the children of God." Instead they insist, in a cauldron of cruelty, "You don't believe what I believe. Therefore, you're not a Christian." I often slump breathless into my chair when a fundamentalist or evangelical says I'm damned simply because I do not share the same beliefs and have a different conception of God and Jesus.

This kind of intolerance sent me into a heartbreaking crisis. In a bathtub of tears, I finally realized that only when we

tolerate the intolerant

and love the cold-hearted can we truly know God—and truly understand what it means to be a Christian. As Rabbi Michael Lerner writes, no worthwhile goal "justifies demeaning the humanity and ignoring the spirit of God in those with whom we disagree." And so I send my love to all—especially to those with whom I disagree.

At least a hundred years after Jesus' death, an enormously gifted, anonymous poet put these words into Jesus' mouth: "I am the way and the truth and the life. No one comes to the Father except through me" (John 14:6). Scholars now agree that the historical Jesus could not possibly have said this.* But even if Jesus did say it, we know that "the way" that Jesus taught is **inclusive**, not exclusive; **forgiving**, not condemning; born of **peace**, not war. The one true way of the Cosmic Christ is to find a way in your heart to **include people of other ways**. The "one true way" is to say, "I love you." Not, "You're damned and going to hell because you don't believe as I believe."

*"There is scarcely a single competent New Testament scholar who is prepared to defend the view that the four instances of the absolute use of 'I am' in John, or indeed most of the other uses, can be historically attributed to Jesus," writes Bible scholar Adrian Thatcher.

A burgeoning number of Protestant denominations are rejecting the bigotry of the past and embracing a profoundly **ecumenical spirit**. The National Council of Churches (NCC) General Assembly recently published a landmark policy statement called "Interfaith Relations and the Churches." "As Christians we recognize that Jesus is not central to other religious traditions. For men and women in other communities,

the mystery of God

takes many forms," the statement reads. "Because God is at work in all creation, we can expect to find new understanding of our faith through **dialogue** with people of other religions."

The NCC proclamation builds on the Nostra Aetate of 1965, perhaps the greatest document ever produced by the Vatican. Regarding Judaism, Buddhism, Hinduism and Islam, "The Catholic Church rejects nothing of what is true and holy in these religions. It has high regard for the manner of life and conduct, the precepts and doctrines which, although differing in many ways from its own teaching, nevertheless often reflect a ray of truth that enlightens all men and women."

This kind of language must come from people of all denominations and all faiths if there be any hope for mankind.

"WE HUMAN BEINGS CAN BE NOURISHED BY THE BEST VALUES OF MANY TRADITIONS."

THICH NHAT HANH

Many Jews have never read the Christian Testament; Orthodox Jews are even forbidden from reading it. "Those who read the Christian Testament will have no portion in the world to come," reads a famous passage from the Talmud (Sanhedrin 90a). Yet just about all of the teachings of Jesus are derived from the Torah, the Jewish prophetic writings, and the vast oral tradition of the Israelites.

As Paul wrote in Galatians 1:16, he discovered Jesus "in me." Paul, a zealous Rabbi who hated and persecuted the Christians, suddenly found the love of the Cosmic Christ burning hot inside his heart. The Greek of his letter to the Galatians is clear about this. Paul discovered the Cosmic Christ not physically outside of him, but **within him**. Likewise, you can discover this love, this inner source of joy and peace, pulsing like a geyser through your heart.

George Lakoff wrote a wonderful book called, Don't Think of an Elephant. The idea is that when someone tells you not to think of an elephant, right away you think of an elephant. When someone claims that Jesus was born of a virgin and raised bodily from the dead, you should not assume that all Christians believe this, or that Christianity has no value without such beliefs. Never let others define how you think about God and spirituality. Jesus simply teaches this:

look

beyond the strangeness

of others and probe for **pearls** of the heart.

Because I was born Jewish and am so inspired by the Cosmic Christ as a spiritual ideal, people sometimes mistakenly label me as a "Messianic Jew" or a "Jew for Jesus." I reviewed their doctrinal statements and found that I do not believe any of them. Jesus was obviously not the Jewish Messiah because the Messiah was supposed to usher in an era of world peace and prosperity. Throughout history, even the idea of an individual Messiah has proven itself to be polarizing and divisive. The Reformed Jewish view is much more resonant for our times: no one individual will ever lord over us or redeem us; but if enough people come together, we can usher in a "Messianic Age" of **pluralism**, **empathy**, **peace**, **love** and **forgiveness**.

The great Jewish theologian Martin Buber said of Jesus, "My own fraternally open relationship to him has grown even stronger and clearer, and today I see him more strongly and clearly than ever before." Although a devout Jew in his own profound and unique way, Buber would **never** have called himself a "Jew for Jesus"; he was not "doctrinaire." He set a magnificent example of how Jews can retain their identity while still expressing an admiration for the

ideals of neighbor love

and heart transformation to which Jesus gave birth. Mark repeatedly shows that the Jesus of history took great pains **not to identify** himself as the Messiah or to proclaim himself divine.

25

The historical Jesus had a profound appreciation for the sacred, old and new. He honored his Jewish tradition but he never pandered to it in the way that many pander to the tradition that bears his name. He boldly declared that the meek, the lonely and the lost in spirit are sacred. He declared that tax collectors and prostitutes are sacred. He taught us not so much what is sacred but that **each of us has the joyous capacity to declare what is sacred**, once we cleanse ourselves of anger and anxiety and get in touch with our Divine Source. As Whitman said,

> **Divine am** I inside and out,
> and **I make holy** whatever I touch.

Scholars are helping us to rediscover

ſlong loſt dimensions

of the sacred, some of which were suppressed by the Church fathers and some of which were lost during the Enlightenment. As Elaine Pagels explains in her marvelous book, **Beyond Belief**, the early Christians were not "believers" as we understand the term today. Many of the early Christians "saw themselves not so much as believers but as **seekers**." But starting with the Gospel of John (written about 70 years after the death of Jesus) and culminating with the Nicene Creed in the fourth century, to be a Christian became conflated with what you believed. To this day, we describe Christians as "believers" and mistakenly exclude from the Church millions of people with loving Christian hearts, simply because of their beliefs.

You can enjoy reading the Bible and the Bhagavad Gita—but this does not mean that you need to believe them literally, as a third millennium reader uses the word "believe." "Belief" implies a scientific, factual understanding of events, many of which simply could not have happened 2,000 years ago. The ancient Latin word for belief was "credo," which really meant, "**I give my heart to.**" Not, "I believe in the facts of."

Our wisdom scriptures are, to borrow an ancient Buddhist phrase, "dark to the mind, but radiant to the heart." The world desperately needs interpretations of Scripture that are radiant to the heart, that do not lose us in the darkness of doctrine. We desperately need scriptures with commentary that encourages love, forgiveness, reconciliation, tolerance and inclusivity, not war, hatred, violence, exclusivity or bigotry. In Mark, especially, scholars are rediscovering many

lost spiritual treasures,
many verses and stories that can still create shivers of awe and recognition within our hearts. They do not explain Creation, but they do deepen our **awareness** of a **Cosmic Power far greater** than our individual egos.

At my local Community Church, we often sing a hymn entitled, "They'll know we are Christians by our love, by our love." The hymn beautifully defines who is a Christian. In fact, there is no better definition of a Christian than this. Yet in our culture, many Christians assert, "They'll know we are Christians by our beliefs, by our beliefs." Such a proclamation is as absurd as it is unhealthy. Your beliefs can never make you a Christian. You know you are a Christian when you discover "how wide and long and high and deep is the love" you feel for God and neighbor, as the anonymous author of Ephesians wrote in verse 3:18.

God said, "Thou shalt love."
God never said, "Thou shalt believe."

One other thing is clear from the Bible. Love is not a choice; it is a commandment. Three times daily, in the original Hebrew, Orthodox Jews recite these great lines from Deuteronomy: "And you shall love the Lord your God with all your heart and all your soul and all your might." How can God command us to love? Is love not voluntary?

I think that God understands our

postmodern predicament

perfectly well and offers a magnificent path to all who have the heart to see it. God commands us to love because, as history proves daily, we are not inclined to love. We have turned our boats into battleships. Of what use is it to say, "I believe in Jesus Christ," but then treat others like sharks, or call Islam a "religion of hate," as numerous Christians do? Homo sapiens need love as a Commandment with a capital C, not an option with a lowercase o. Love is God's absolute moral imperative, not a relative preference for the moment. No matter our science or progress, we still need love.

Beliefs change, our scientific understanding of the world changes, but God's **commandment to love** will never change.

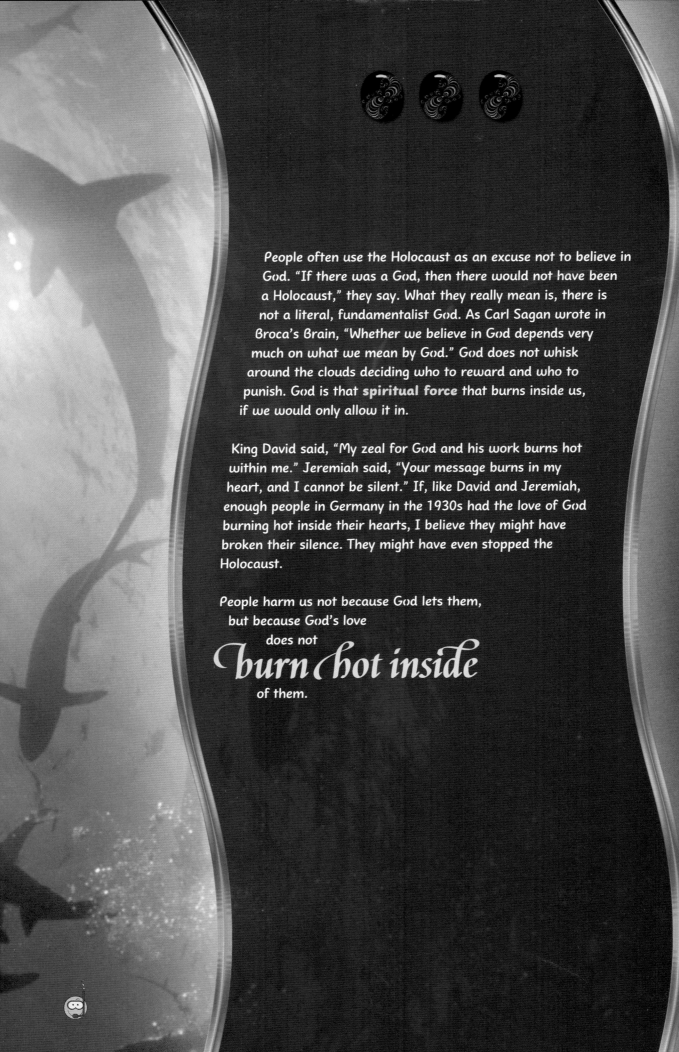

People often use the Holocaust as an excuse not to believe in God. "If there was a God, then there would not have been a Holocaust," they say. What they really mean is, there is not a literal, fundamentalist God. As Carl Sagan wrote in Broca's Brain, "Whether we believe in God depends very much on what we mean by God." God does not whisk around the clouds deciding who to reward and who to punish. God is that **spiritual force** that burns inside us, if we would only allow it in.

King David said, "My zeal for God and his work burns hot within me." Jeremiah said, "Your message burns in my heart, and I cannot be silent." If, like David and Jeremiah, enough people in Germany in the 1930s had the love of God burning hot inside their hearts, I believe they might have broken their silence. They might have even stopped the Holocaust.

People harm us not because God lets them, but because God's love does not

burn hot inside

of them.

One of the best definitions of what it means to love God comes from Harith B. Asad Al-Muhasibi, the great ninth century Sufi mystic: "The love of God in its essence is really the **illumination of the heart by joy.**" Have you ever heard any definition more beautiful than this? Another Sufi mystic, Abu'l-Majdud B.Adam Sanai'I, wrote, "Whatever **increases the brightness of your heart** brings nearer God's manifestation of Himself to you." The Sufi mystics make clear that the love of God is not the love of a dualistic deity or a "divine son." The love of God is, rather, the opening of your heart and the unleashing of your Sacred Energies.

Like the seemingly helpless man in Mark 9:24, we connect with God through an act of humility, an acknowledgement of our frailty and mortality. The mere act of asking for help is the starting point for the connection we seek.

What the father was really saying to Jesus was, "Help me open my heart." In Mark 7:34, in fact, Jesus uses the Aramaic word, ephphatha,

which means,

be opened up!

It is not through scientific belief but through opening our hearts that we find God in the third millennium. Nietzsche was right: the God who was a Cosmic bell captain, the God who supernaturally intervened in the affairs of men, favoring one boat over another on the surface, is dead. But Nietzsche was wrong, too: the God of the heart, the God of the Cosmos who is an infinite Sea of love, who can transform us into higher spiritual beings, is alive and well. And not only alive and well: in a world of conflict and ever more destructive technologies, this God may be **the last great hope for mankind.**

BREATHING IN I SMILE,
BREATHING OUT I RELAX.
THIS IS A WONDERFUL MOMENT.

ROGER WALSH

"SPIRITUAL EPIPHANY... REQUIRES THE
PUTTING ON OF NEW GLASSES — ONES
THAT HELP US TO SEE, IN FULL COLOR AND
OCEAN-LIKE BEAUTY, THE GRACE THAT IS
WRITTEN ALL OVER OUR WORLDS."

DONNA FREITAS

A midrash is a commentary on ancient wisdom, a way of applying it to modern life. The pages that follow are a young woman's midrash on the Cosmic Christ, her heartfelt search for a spirituality that still speaks to us in the third millennium. I write God instead of God and Cosmic instead of Cosmic "to emphasize the inadequacy of our language to speak about the divine," as Elizabeth Schussler Fiorenza puts it. The open o symbolizes

the New openness

with which we are approaching our wisdom traditions. I also created a new letter, ꞌn, and some new words, ꞌne, ꞌnim and ꞌner, when referring to God or the Cosmic Christ as a pronoun, because I believe that God transcends gender and is neither a "she" nor a "he." The ꞌn marries the s and the h; I pronounce it "shah," but how you pronounce it is entirely up to you.

You cannot hear a midrash on the Cosmic Christ from the boat. This is an underwater midrash, a search for sunken treasures of the human heart. You can hear it only when your ears are pressed **close to the mystery** and when you allow your heart to get wet with love.

Much of the commentary in this book draws on scholarship and archeological findings that only recently have become available to the general public. That I have made it this far is nothing less than miraculous. I do not have an encyclopedic knowledge of the Scriptures. I am not a Huston Smith or a Joseph Campbell. By day, I teach at an inner city public school in the Bronx, New York. By night, I buzz from tradition to tradition, a humble bee in a world of giants, collecting bits of pollen and doing my best to convert them into spiritual honey. I find solace in the words of the Sufi mystic Bayazid Bistami: "**God dwells in a humble heart.**" None of us is capable of fully mastering all of the great wisdom traditions in their original languages and historical context, but we are capable of appreciating them with a humble heart, no matter how flawed and imperfect we may be.

The Buddha said, "Do not belittle your virtues, saying, 'they are nothing.' A jug fills drop by drop so the wise person becomes a brimful of virtue." And so, drop by drop, you can gather sweet honeycombs for your soul. Like a Zen Buddhist, you can **let go and let yourself be** in the moment. You can renew yourself with the spirit of a child and the simplicity of the "beginner's mind."

The writer Karen Armstrong, a former Catholic nun, spoke for many of us when she said: "I have drawn nourishment from **Judaism** and **Islam**, as well as from the various forms of **Christianity**. I cannot regard any one of these faiths as superior, and certainly do not regard any one as having the monopoly of truth... My last book was about the **Buddha** and I was quite enthralled by his insights. I am also discovering the **Chinese** traditions, as well as **Hinduism**... At the moment I find inspiration in them all."

Armstrong is emblematic of something profound in the air right now: a new generation of "spiritual chemists" who combine elements from each tradition to create a

New spiritual synthesis
within themselves.

We have already witnessed the beginnings of this new spiritual synthesis, this "**dancing together**" in interfaith charity drives, meetings, seminars, journals and books; with Christians such as Bede Griffiths and Thomas Merton studying Zen meditation; Buddhists such as the Dalai Lama and Thich Nhat Hanh studying the Gospels; Jews such as Rabbi Michael Lerner founding interfaith organizations; and so on. As we will see in the following pages, cultural icons as diverse as the Dalai Lama and Madonna are showing us how to find **joy in many faiths**.

love love love love love
love love love love love
love love love love love

"SEEK OUT THOSE MYSTERIES
DESTINED FOR YOU."

FARID AL-DIN 'ATTAR

"ONLY THAT DAY DAWNS
TO WHICH WE ARE AWAKE."

HENRY DAVID THOREAU

Here you will discover how little the Jesus of the Gospels has to do with the Jesus of American politics. In his bestselling book, God's Politics, the evangelical Christian Jim Wallis writes, "Many of us feel that our faith has been stolen, and it's time to take it back. In particular, an enormous public misrepresentation of Christianity has taken place. And because of an almost uniform media misperception, many people around the world now think Christian faith stands for political commitments that are almost the opposite of its true meaning."

No translation on the market today gets you closer to this true meaning than the Scholars Version, first published in 1992 by the Westar Institute. A landmark collaboration of top scholars from Harvard, Vassar, Notre Dame and other major universities, it is the first major English translation **"free of ecclesiastical and religious control, unlike other major translations into English,"** states Robert W. Funk, the founder of the Jesus Seminar. The Scholars Version of the Gospel of Mark is presented here, unabridged. Most people do not realize that Mark writes his Gospel in the present tense. In Mark, there is often no distinction between past, present and future; he uses the Greek historical present over 150 times. The Scholars Version remains the only major contemporary translation that accurately restores the present tense to Mark.

Mark writes in the **present tense** for a profound reason. He never intends his Gospel as dogma or doctrine. He provides a spiritual launching pad, speaking to us not as first century Romans but as third millennium spiritual pilgrims. As Matthew Fox says, our world yearns for an era of unsurpassed spiritual creativity "that can be experienced if we dare to

Awaken the mystic within

ourselves and our traditions."
The mystic is awakened in the present; the Scholars Version is a beautiful launching pad for such a journey.

"When you appreciate the beauty and uniqueness of things, you receive energy," writes James Redfield in his spiritual thriller, **The Celestine Prophecy**. "The perception of beauty is a kind of barometer telling each of us how close we are to actually perceiving the energy." If you have ever tried to define beauty, or wondered why beauty is essential to human spirituality, Redfield has revealed the secret: Beauty is a gateway to the **energy of God**.

The pages that follow help you to open your heart to this energy. They are a kind of **visual yoga**, helping your mind to stretch and then settle into silence. The fractal art symbolizes the energy fields and spiritual planes of which we are all a part. Each fractal is a channel into the infinite, a way of visualizing the spiritual waves and vibrations which, until very recently, were hidden from view.

Each of the twelve metallic inks invites you to explore a different energy field. They remind you of your metallic origins —for you are literally made of **stardust**—and of the **presence** of God literally within you.

We are now discovering that this energy we call God evolves and expands as the Universe **evolves and expands**. The Universe is becoming aware of itself through us. Art plays a critical role by providing a nonverbal, nonlinear path to this

New Cosmic Awareness.

The deeper truths of our wisdom traditions cannot be expressed verbally, least of all through dogma or doctrine. The artwork invites you to dive into the mystery, to discover the divine energy within yourself and throughout all of God's magnificent creations.

"PEACE IS THE FIRST GLIMPSE
OF THE INNER KINGDOM OF GOD."

PARAMAHANSA YOGANANDA

ACCORDING TO MARK

The Lost Spiritual World series begins with Mark because the scholarly consensus is now that Mark's Gospel — not Matthew's — is the first account of the life and teachings of Jesus ever written. Both Protestant and Catholic authorities refused to take the Gospel of Mark seriously until the 19th century. They mistakenly claimed, like Augustine, that Mark is little more than a poorly written rehash of Matthew. They ignored Mark because he **makes no mention** of giving Peter the "keys to the kingdom"; **provides no justification** for the legitimacy of the Roman Catholic Church; **never gives** an account of the Resurrection; **never mentions** the Trinity; and **never claims** that Jesus was born of a virgin.

Mark fascinates us today precisely because he reveals — some say revels in — the

flawed, humble, human

Jesus and his disciples. The oldest manuscripts are known only as ΚΑΤΑ ΜΑΡΚΟΝ, meaning "according to Mark," not "the Gospel of Mark." The shift in emphasis is profound: "according to" reminds us that this is Mark's perspective, one of many; whereas the "Gospel of" implies a canonical stability which **emerged only much later** in Church history. The earliest surviving manuscripts of the other canonical Gospels are likewise known as, "According to Luke," "According to Matthew" and "According to John."

In the illuminated manuscripts of medieval times, the lion symbolized Mark's Gospel. Artists were inspired by his portrait of John the Baptist, "the voice of one roaring in the wilderness." Here the lion rests his paw on a computer and lets loose a friendly roar, symbolizing the **rediscovery** of a lost spiritual world and the **birth** of a beautiful new one.

http://www.lostspiritualworld.com

enter

MIDRASH:
A CHANGE OF HEART

42

The Talmud tells the story of a convert to Judaism who asked the great Rabbi Hillel to "teach me the whole of the Torah while I stand on one leg." The Rabbi said, "**Love** your neighbor as yourself. The rest is commentary."* Likewise, if many of us were asked to summarize the Christian faith in a single sentence, we might respond, "Change your heart. The rest is commentary."

Most Bible commentaries (and bitter arguments) on the beginning of Mark's Gospel focus on theological concepts, such as baptism, repentance, whether Jesus was literally the son of God, or whether the doctrine of original sin can be derived from this passage. But **beautifully and simply**, Mark reveals the essence of the Christian faith in verse 4: change your heart.

The rest of Mark's Gospel is simply a bonus, simply commentary. Even if you never read another word of the Bible again, if you just remember these three words, you will be an

Angel in God's eyes.

*(Bavli Shabbat 31a)

http://www.heart.change

Mark 1: 1-11

¹THE GOOD NEWS OF JESUS THE ANOINTED

begins ²with something Isaiah the prophet wrote: Here is my messenger, whom I send on ahead of you to prepare your way! ³A voice of someone shouting in the wilderness: "Make ready the way of the Lord, make his paths straight." ⁴So, John the Baptizer appeared in the wilderness calling for baptism and a

CHANGE OF HEART

that lead to **FORGIVENESS** of sins. ⁵And everyone from the Judean countryside and all the residents of Jerusalem streamed out to him and got baptized by him in the Jordan river, admitting their sins. ⁶And John wore a mantle made of camel hair and had a leather belt around his waist and lived on locusts and raw honey. ⁷And he began his proclamation by saying: "Someone more powerful than I will succeed me, whose sandal straps I am not fit to bend down and untie. ⁸I have been baptizing you with water, but he will baptize you with holy spirit." ⁹During that same period Jesus came from Nazareth, Galilee, and was baptized in the Jordan by John. ¹⁰And just as he got up out of the water, he saw the skies torn open and the spirit coming down toward him like a dove. ¹¹There was also a voice from the skies: "You are my favored son — I fully approve of you."

12:00 AM

Mark 1: 12-20 http://www.darkenergy.trust

¹²AND **RIGHT AWAY** THE SPIRIT **DRIVES** him out into the wilderness, ¹³where he remained for forty days, being put to the test by Satan. While he was living there among the wild animals, the heavenly messengers looked after him. ¹⁴After John was locked up, Jesus came to Galilee proclaiming God's good news. ¹⁵His message went: "The time is up: God's imperial rule is closing in. Change your ways, and put your

TRUST

in the good news!" ¹⁶As he was walking along by the Sea of Galilee, he spotted Simon and Andrew, Simon's brother, casting (their nets) into the sea — since they were fishermen — ¹⁷and Jesus said to them: "Become my followers and I'll have you fishing for people!" ¹⁸And right then and there they abandoned their nets and followed him. ¹⁹When he had gone a little farther, he caught sight of James, Zebedee's son, and his brother John mending their nets in the boat. ²⁰Right then and there he called out to them as well, and they left their father Zebedee behind in the boat with the hired hands and accompanied him.

MIDRASH:
SPIRITUAL WEIGHT LIFTING

Most medieval and Renaissance artists painted the temptation scene literally, showing a monstrous winged creature with pointed ears and black teeth trying to lead Jesus astray. But in a single word, Mark provides a magnificent escape from literalism: **trust**. Trust that temptation can be your friend, if you conquer it. As **Nietzsche** famously said, "What does not destroy me makes me stronger." Nietzsche recognized the value of the Satan **metaphor**—not to cause evil in the world, but to strengthen the good.

Temptation is weight lifting for your soul;
each encounter
builds your

Spiritual Muscles

and deepens your capacity to trust.

The **Dalai Lama** says, "If you can cultivate the right attitude, your enemies are your best spiritual teachers because their presence provides you with the opportunity to enhance and develop tolerance, patience and understanding."

MIDRASH:

SPIRITUAL EXOUSIA

The Greek word for authority is ἐξουσία (exousia). It means "to have an unusual knowledge and power." The scribes derived their authority from laws and traditions. But like the Buddha and Lao Tzu, Jesus derived his authority from within. He had an unusual ability to tap directly into **Source Energy** and to

⸬unleash its power

for the greater good.

The heart of Jesus' teachings is that you can learn to **access this power and exousia within yourself**—and without believing in any of the doctrines. Jesus taught that you can move mountains, transform your entire life through a single act of trust, heal yourself and heal others by tapping into the same exousia he tapped into. He even said that if you have enough faith, "you can surpass all that I have done" (John 14:12).

http://www.exousia.spirit **Mark 1: 21-28**

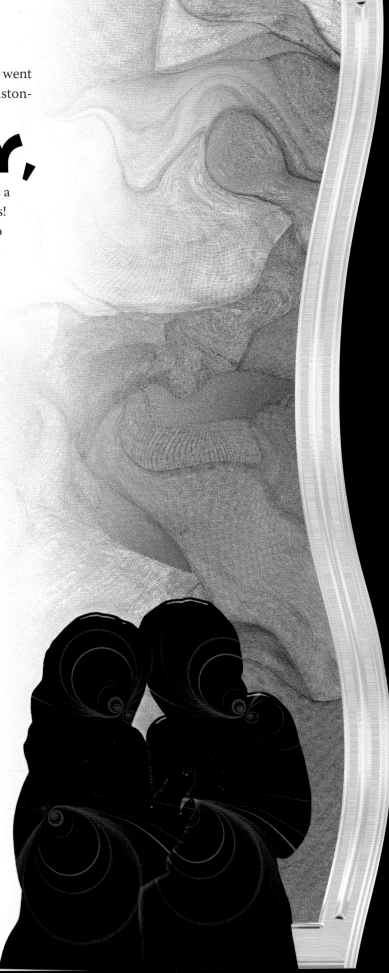

[21]Then they come to Capernaum, and on the sabbath day he went right to the synagogue and started teaching. [22]They were astonished at his teaching, since he would teach them on his own

AUTHORITY,

unlike the scholars. [23]Now right there in their synagogue was a person possessed by an unclean spirit, which shouted, [24]"Jesus! What do you want with us, you Nazarene? Have you come to get rid of us? I know you, who you are: God's holy man!" [25]But Jesus yelled at it, "Shut up and get out of him!" [26]Then the unclean spirit threw the man into convulsions, and letting out a loud shriek it came out of him. [27]And they were all so

AMAZED

that they asked themselves, "What's this? A new kind of teaching backed by authority! He gives orders even to unclean spirits and they obey him!" [28]So his fame spread rapidly everywhere throughout Galilee and even beyond.

Life   Edit   Meditate   Tools   Help

| Mark 1: 29-39 | http://www.music.mind |

[29]They left the synagogue **RIGHT AWAY** and entered the house of Simon and Andrew along with James and John. [30]Simon's mother-in-law was in bed with a fever, and they told him about her right away. [31]He went up to her, took hold of her hand, raised her up, and the fever disappeared. Then she started looking after them. [32]In the evening, at sundown, they would bring all the sick and demon possessed to him. [33]And the whole town would crowd around the door. [34]On such occasions he cured many people afflicted with various diseases and drove out many demons. He would never let the demons speak, because they realized who he was. [35]And rising early, while it was still very dark, he went outside and stole

AWAY TO AN ISOLATED PLACE, WHERE HE STARTED

PRAYING.

[36]Then Simon and those with him hunted him down. [37]When they had found him they say to him, "They're all looking for you." [38]But he replies: "Let's go somewhere else, to the neighboring villages, so I can speak there too, since that's what I came for." [39]So he went all around Galilee speaking in their synagogues and driving out demons.

MIDRASH:
THE NEW MUSIC OF THE MIND

From the late Middle Ages to the Renaissance, Books of Hours—not the Bible—were the world's bestsellers. Books of Hours were beautifully hand-painted prayer books. Their combination of sensuous artwork and pious prayers to Jesus' mother Mary created **a new spiritual experience**, a new way of transcending the tumults of daily life. Readers would escape for a few moments to a quiet place, dip into the lavishly illustrated pages, recite a few Psalms and commune with God.

But you probably no longer see God as a bearded patriarch or a cosmic bell captain who answers prayers with divine intervention. That means you need to refine your understanding of prayer if it is to have any value for you.

A new generation of spiritual teachers is reviving and transforming two ancient practices that are similar to prayer: **meditation and affirmations**. Always recited in the present tense, affirmations are how you actively engage with the **Quantum Field of Possibilities**—God—and commit yourself to a life of greater purpose. Affirmations are how you fully realize the

Power of Now,
as Eckhart Tolle

puts it. Affirmations are the Akashik records of your soul, the tablets of destiny inscribed within your heart.

Affirmations, whose roots we can trace to the ancient mantras of Hinduism and Buddhism, are especially helpful to those who prefer to call themselves "**spiritual** but not religious," those who rarely pray anyway. Louise Hay, one of the pioneers of beautifully illustrated books of affirmations, has published a number of inspiring titles, including **I Can Do It** and **Power Thoughts**. They are to the third millennium what Books of Hours were to the second.

ALPHA   THETA   DELTA   GAMMA

There are many different forms of meditation, but one of the most effective (and best ways to begin) is called "hemispheric synchronization." Scientists have found that if you listen to a signal of one frequency in one ear, and another signal in the other ear, your brain reconciles the difference and creates a new signal, called a binaural beat. During normal conscious awareness, your brain typically resonates in the beta state, which can often be harried, distracted, stressed and frazzled. Binaural beats help you to get out of this beta state and move into the more soothing,

peaceful, transcendent

states of alpha, theta
and delta brainwaves.

The technology can literally give birth to new dendrites and synaptic **connections within your brain.** "Eventually the brain evolves to a point where it is able to perceive, experience, and be one with the interconnections of the entire Universe, allowing the release and healing of addictive and dysfunctional patterns and the growth of an internal sense of peace with oneself and with one's world," explains Bill Harris, creator of the Holosync meditation program.

My favorite compositions are called Sacred Ground, Deep Insight and Increase Creativity, created by Kelly Howell and Robert Schwimmer. Kelly humbly calls them "brain wave audio programs," but I call them Symphonies of the Mind. They are deep explorations of the Inner Cosmos, taking you on a journey that no one, until now, could ever experience.

You can even combine your affirmations with the new brain music. With an iPod in your shirt pocket, you can escape to a quiet place, put on your headphones, close your eyes and tune into the Infinite.

Whether you prefer meditation to prayer, or mantras to affirmations, is secondary to a much deeper issue facing our culture today. From the ancient wisdom traditions to the bleeding edge of science, you are reminded of the importance—many would say the absolute necessity—of

stilling your Mind,

of finding peace without drugs or alcohol or overeating or anything that might hinder your path to Spiritual Enlightenment.

As Paramahansa Yogananda writes, "Unwillingness to meditate should be recognized as among the foremost enemies of man's physical, mental and spiritual well-being... When man is master of himself—moderate, calm, understanding, unselfish, forgiving, practicing meditation—he is inviting God to help him."

The historical Jesus never owned an iPod and never had his brain wired for biofeedback. But the ideals which he espoused—**peace**, **love**, **reconciliation**, **inclusivity** and **forgiveness**—are realized especially in group meditation and group prayer. In 1993, for what was called the Transcendental Meditation Program, 4,000 people gathered for two months in Washington, D.C. to meditate for peace. During this time, researchers documented a 48% reduction in violent crimes such as homicide, rape, aggravated assault and robbery in the District of Columbia.

Science is now confirming that when we meditate or pray **together**, we can bring peace not only to ourselves but also to entire communities, entire nations—even to the world.

At left:
Jesus listening to his iPod.

51

Life **Edit** Cleanse Tools Help

- Fear
- Doubt
- Anxiety
- Uncertainty
- Loneliness
- Depression
- Nervousness
- Resistence
- Show Hidden

Mark

http://www.energy.source

[40]Then a leper comes up to him, pleads with him, falls down on his knees, and says to him, "If you want to, you can make me clean." [41]Although Jesus was indignant, he stretched out his hand, touched him, and says to him, "Okay— you're clean!" [42]And right away the leprosy disappeared, and he was made

CLEAN.

[43]And Jesus snapped at him, and dismissed him curtly [44]with this warning: "See that you don't tell anyone anything, but go, have a priest examine (your skin). Then offer for your cleansing what Moses commanded, as evidence (of your cure)." [45]But after he left, he started telling everyone and spreading the story, so that (Jesus) could no longer enter a town openly, but had to stay out in the countryside. Yet they continued to come to him from everywhere.

12:54 AM

In Greek, the man was a "lepros," which meant that he could have either been a leper or someone with a skin disease. In this context, he clearly had a skin disease, but the undercurrent of a more insidious disease is fascinating.

The man may have felt ugly, fearing that his skin disease made him repugnant to others. You often need a friend or an "anointed one" to whisper these precious words of encouragement into your ears: you are clean, you are beautiful,

you are a child of god.

In the third millennium, we've cured ourselves of physical leprosy, but not **spiritual leprosy**. Our doubts, fears and anxieties are all forms of spiritual leprosy. We too often go through life saying to ourselves, "I am a leper," when in fact we only have scabby skin, and this is either of little consequence or can be cured.

In his classic book, Psychocybernetics, Maxwell Maltz tells of a nose job he performed on a woman. Maltz did an especially fine job and proudly lifted a mirror to her eyes to showcase her beautiful new nose. The woman complained that she saw no improvement. It turns out that her real problem was not her nose, but her self-esteem. The Cosmic Christ says to us, "You are not a leper. You are a really beautiful person, just as you are. **Have faith in yourself,** as I have faith in you."

 SPIRITUAL ROOTS

The Greek word for cleansed is καθαρίσ, from which we get the word catharsis. The Gospel writers were profoundly aware of the impact that a deep spiritual cleansing — a "catharsis" — can have on our physical healing.

Life   Edit   Ecstasy   Tools   Help

Mark 2: 1-12   http://www.zeropoint.ecstasy

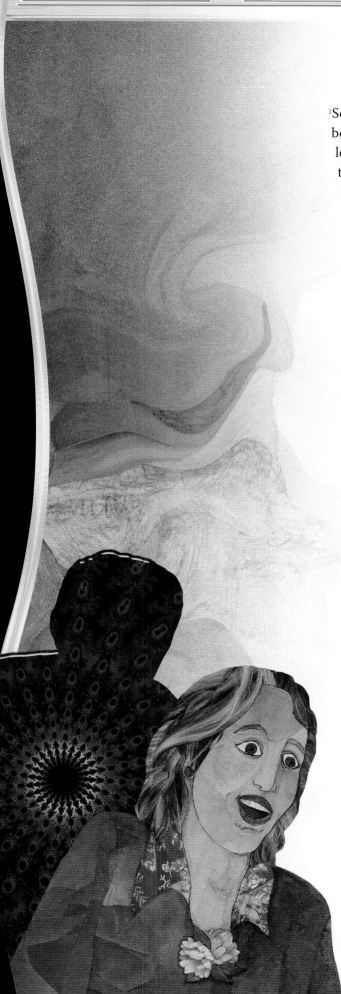

[1]Some days later he went back to Capernaum and was rumored to be at home. [2]And many people crowded around so there was no longer any room, even outside the door. Then he started speaking to them. [3]Some people then show up with a paralytic being carried by four of them. [4]And when they were not able to get near him on account of the crowd, they removed the roof above him. After digging it out, they lowered the mat on which the paralytic was lying. [5]When Jesus noticed their **TRUST**, he says to the paralytic, "Child, your sins are forgiven." [6]Some of the scholars were sitting there and silently wondering:[7]"Why does that fellow say such things? He's blaspheming! Who can forgive sins except the one God?" [8]And **RIGHT AWAY**, because Jesus sensed in his spirit that they were raising questions like this among themselves, he says to them: "Why do you entertain questions about these things? [9]Which is easier, to say to the paralytic, 'Your sins are forgiven,' or to say, 'Get up, pick up your mat and walk'?" [10]But so that you may realize that on earth the son of Adam has authority to forgive sins, he says to the paralytic, [11]"You there, get up, pick up your mat and go home!" [12]And he got up, picked his mat right up, and walked out as everyone looked on. So they all became

ECSTATIC

extolled God, and exclaimed,

"WE'VE **NEVER SEEN** THE LIKES OF THIS!"

MIDRASH:
THE MIRACLE OF METAPHOR

"There are only two ways to live your life.
One is as though nothing is a **miracle**.
The other is as though everything is a **miracle**."

Albert Einstein

Jesus was a master of metaphor just as Magritte was a master of mystique. He was remarkably aware of how metaphor impacts your spirituality. He freely admits in John 16:25, "I have spoken to you in figures of speech." His exousia, his authority in the third millennium comes from his showing you how to **transform your metaphors**.

Jesus changed the metaphors of the paralytic from, "You are a sinner" to "You are forgiven." From "You are sick" to "You are healed." He intuitively understood what modern science has affirmed over and over: your psychological state has an enormous impact on your physical state—and can even cause paralysis.

When you feel
emotionally paralyzed
you often cannot pinpoint in words the source of the paralysis. This is where the metaphors of the Cosmic Christ say, "You can do it. You are healed right now. Now get up and walk, you angel, you."

We humans have a deep need to connect in some way with

the inexplicable mystery

of why we are here.

The early Christian writers often had no other way of getting us closer to the presence of God than through metaphor. To borrow a phrase from Paul, metaphor "makes known the invisible things of God" (Romans 1:20). It allows you to visualize the spiritual, to synchronize the flow of your emotions to the flow of life.

The great theologian of the Middle Ages, Thomas Aquinas, had a much deeper understanding of metaphor than the literalists of our day. "We truly know God when we trust that He is **far beyond** all that man can possibly think of." Literalism restricts and perverts how we think of God by asserting that the Bible is literal truth—not metaphorical truth, as Aquinas rightly understood.

Literalist creeds assert the letter of the law, while metaphorical readings **capture its progressive spirit.** As Paul said, we should follow not of the letter of our Scriptures, but the spirit; "for the letter kills, but the spirit gives life" (2 Corinthians 3:6). Even Oswald Chambers, who is the favored theologian of many American evangelicals and fundamentalists today (including President Bush), writes, "When we become advocates of a creed, something dies; we do not believe God, we only believe our belief about him" (See "My Utmost For His Highest," April 29th).

The theologian Paul Tillich said, "Literalism deprives God of his ultimacy and, religiously speaking, of his majesty. It draws him down to the level of that which is not ultimate, the finite and conditional." The mythologist Joseph Campbell said, "When you let the literal meaning of a religious tradition die, then it **comes alive again.**"

2:36 AM

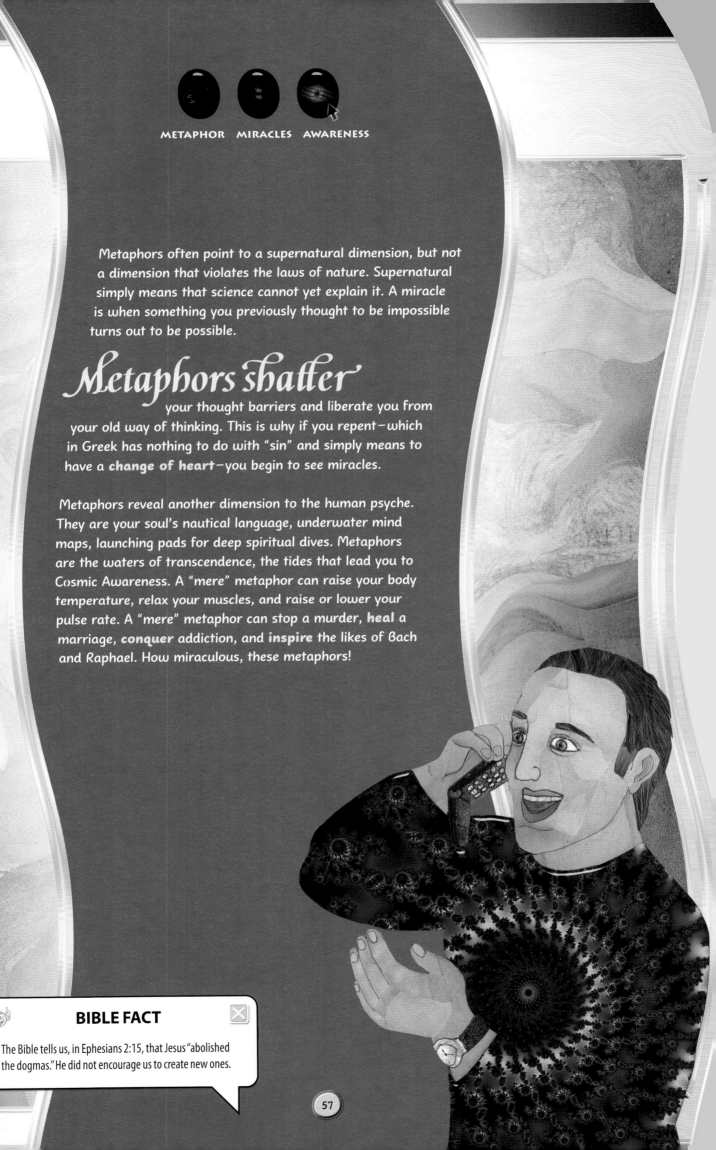

Metaphors often point to a supernatural dimension, but not a dimension that violates the laws of nature. Supernatural simply means that science cannot yet explain it. A miracle is when something you previously thought to be impossible turns out to be possible.

Metaphors shatter

your thought barriers and liberate you from your old way of thinking. This is why if you repent—which in Greek has nothing to do with "sin" and simply means to have a **change of heart**—you begin to see miracles.

Metaphors reveal another dimension to the human psyche. They are your soul's nautical language, underwater mind maps, launching pads for deep spiritual dives. Metaphors are the waters of transcendence, the tides that lead you to Cosmic Awareness. A "mere" metaphor can raise your body temperature, relax your muscles, and raise or lower your pulse rate. A "mere" metaphor can stop a murder, **heal** a marriage, **conquer** addiction, and **inspire** the likes of Bach and Raphael. How miraculous, these metaphors!

BIBLE FACT

The Bible tells us, in Ephesians 2:15, that Jesus "abolished the dogmas." He did not encourage us to create new ones.

Life   Edit   Liberate   Tools   Help

Mark 2: 13-17   http://www.thumbprint.god

[13]Again he went out by the sea. And, with a huge crowd gathered around him, he started teaching. [14]As he was walking along, he caught sight of Levi, the son of Alphaeus, sitting at the toll booth, and he says to him, "Follow me!" And Levi got up and followed him. [15]Then Jesus happens to recline at table in (Levi's) house, along with many toll collectors and sinners and Jesus' disciples. (Remember, there were many of these people and they were all following him.) [16]And whenever the Pharisees' scholars saw him eating with sinners and toll collectors, they would question his disciples: "What's he doing eating with toll collectors and sinners?" [17]When Jesus overhears, he says to them: "Since when do the able-bodied need a doctor? It's the sick who do.

I DID NOT
COME TO ENLIST
RELIGIOUS FOLKS

but sinners!"

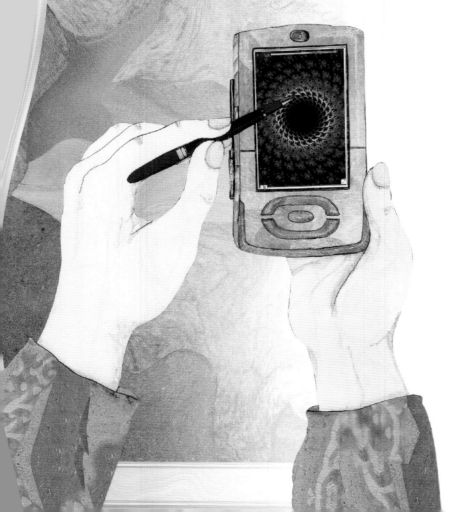

MIDRASH:

SPIRITUAL, NOT RELIGIOUS

Mark 2:17 is a critically important verse because Jesus refutes two common misconceptions about his ministry. First, when he says, "I did not come to enlist religious folks," he makes clear that his ministry is **not universal** and that **not everyone** needs him. Second, he did not come to argue dogma or doctrine, but to minister

as a

spiritual doctor

to people in need.

The Greek word for sin is ἁμαρτία (hamartia), an archery term which originally meant "to miss the target." Read Mark carefully: Jesus **never** proclaims that "we are all sinners." If anything, he sought to release us from the dreadful metaphor of sin. In fact, in the Gospel of Mary (3:2), Peter asks Jesus, "What is the sin of the world?" And Jesus answers, "**There is no such thing as sin.**"

As a Jew, Jesus most definitely could not have believed in the doctrine of "original sin." Augustine formulated that doctrine in his book, The City of God, written four hundred years after Jesus' death. Jesus was much closer in his beliefs to the Buddhist monk Thich Nhat Hanh, who said, "We do not speak about original sin in Buddhism, but we do talk about negative seeds that exist in every person—seeds of **hatred, anger, ignorance, intolerance**, and so on—and we say that these seeds can be transformed when we touch the qualities of a Buddha, which are also seeds within us."

In her spiritual classic, A Course in Miracles, Helen Schulman writes, "**Sin is lack of love.**" In two thousand years, no one has offered a better definition of sin than this.

BIBLE FACT

In Mark 2:17, Jesus says he "did not come to enlist religious folks."

Mark 2: 18-22   http://www.spiritual.waves

[18]John's disciples and the Pharisees were in the habit of fasting, and they come and ask him, "Why do the disciples of John fast, and the disciples of the Pharisees, but your disciples don't?" [19]And Jesus said to them: "The groom's friends can't fast while the groom is around, can they? So long as the groom is around, you can't expect them to fast. [20]But the days will come when the groom is taken away from them, and then they will fast, on that day. [21]"Nobody sews a piece of unshrunk cloth on an old garment, otherwise the new, unshrunk patch pulls away from the old and creates a worse tear. [22]"And nobody pours young wine into old wineskins, otherwise the wine will burst the skins, and destroy both the wine and the skins. Instead,

YOUNG WINE IS FOR NEW WINESKINS."

MIDRASH:

SPIRITUAL WAVES

"He who takes the straight path bounces up and down."
Lao Tzu (Tao Te Ching 41)

In the second century, one of the fathers of the Church, Irenaeus, led the effort to create an official, unchangeable canon of Christian knowledge. He was very uncomfortable with diverse viewpoints and competing schools of thought, which threatened his authority as bishop of Lyon in France. He despised the Valentianian Christians, a deeply spiritual, nonviolent, egalitarian group within early Christianity. Their idea that the Kingdom of God is found **within the human heart**, as the Gospel of Thomas had so beautifully stated (and not in a formal political power structure), was anathema to Irenaeus.

Irenaeus' famous surviving book is a polemic entitled, Against Choice. Both words are revealing: Irenaeus stood, above all, not for something but against something. He and Ignatius of Antioch turned the Latin word for choice, "**heresy**," into a dirty word. Soon any **choice** that did not conform to what the early Church fathers believed was called a theological error—even a "sin."

Irenaeus coined a word to describe his views of the emerging Christian canon of texts: "**orthodox**," which in Greek literally meant "**straight thinking**." With his new word and "straight thinking" views he quashed some of the deepest, most beautiful, most mystical aspects of Christianity. Contrary to what Jesus himself taught in Mark 2:22, Matthew 9:17 and Luke 5:37, there would be no new wine, no new wineskins, no new ways of interpreting and experiencing Christ—not if Irenaeus could help it. The magnificent *early spiritual world* of Christianity—a world of twists and turns and zigs and zags and whirls and waves—was mostly lost until the remarkable discovery in 1945 of the Nag Hammadi library, one of the treasures of the early church.

By the fourth century, an influential bishop of Alexandria named Athanasius encouraged his fellow Christians to codify a "**canon**" of 27 officially approved texts called "the New Testament." In English, a canon is "a set of authoritative religious writings." But in Greek, kanon originally meant "**straight edge**." It is peculiar that Irenaeus, Athanasius and Eusebius used words such as "canon" and "orthodox." What was—and what continues to be for some—the appeal of the "straight" to the **exclusion** of the wavy?

Paul wrote of "the peace that surpasses all understanding." Yet the so-called "straight thinking" doctrines—the canonical, orthodox doctrines—insist in precise detail how you are supposed to understand this peaceful relationship with the Cosmic Christ. With the exclusivist Nicene Creed and all the male-created doctrines ever since, the **peace** of which Paul spoke was **lost** for those who cannot experience the Cosmic Christ in quite the same way.

As Karen King, a professor at Harvard Divinity School, writes, "One consequence of the triumph of Nicene orthodoxy was that the viewpoints of other Christians were largely **lost**, surviving only in documents denouncing them. Until now. The clearest contribution of the recent discoveries is in providing a wealth of primary works that illustrate

the plural character

of early Christianity and offer alternative voices. They disclose a much more diverse Christianity than we had ever suspected."

One of the most misinterpreted lines in the New Testament is John 14:6: "Straight is the gate, and narrow is the way, that leads to life, and few find it." What kind of cruel God would want only a few to find the way? In the Gospel of Thomas, Jesus makes clear that God wants all of us to find the Way, **the unique spiritual wave within ourselves** (Thomas 70). This is what our wisdom traditions do at their best: they bring forth the Divine Self capable of loving even its enemies, something Church Father Irenaeus simply could not do.

RHYTHM **FLOW**

63

John 14:6 highlights the need to move away from literal-ism and develop fresh interpretations of verses which have caused millions of people to burn at the stake in the name of God and Jesus Christ. Science has proven that Irenaeus' straight and narrow view of the world was born of igno-rance. **Sound** travels in waves; **light** is both a particle and a wave; and even **time** and **space** bend, as Einstein showed.

Peer into the music of Bach and Mozart on a computer screen. You will see that **music of the heart**—God's music —is created only with waves. The waves reveal God as a verb, an experience of the sacred flow and rhythm of life. The straight line is cold, Newtonian, mechanical, reductionist, materialist, fundamentalist. The waves are joyful, mystical and beautifully inexplicable.

The straight and narrow, fundamentalist, black and white view of the world denies these waves, tries to repress and suppress them in the name of a single, orthodox, superior viewpoint which condemns and excludes all others. The waves

include and interweave

a diversity of viewpoints. The waves build consensus; the straight line ignores it. The waves flow; the straight line forces. The waves **unite**; the straight line divides. The waves say: for thousands of years, you have been thinking one way; now think another. Nothing less than the

future of humanity

is at stake given our technologies of mass destruction and our continued inability to live in **peace**. As Einstein famously said, "Problems that are created by our current level of thinking can't be solved by the same level of thinking." The kind of orthodox "straight thinking" exhibited by Irenaeus—which haunts us to this day —simply cannot continue if our planet is to survive.

EMERGE   CREATE

Your atoms, cells, molecules, DNA: all communicate through waves. You are literally a beacon of resonating waves that speaks to the universe through your own unique spiritual frequency, interconnected with all the other frequencies.

No matter how much you magnify or study the waves, you still see new patterns and images emerging, because the great frontier, the essence of God, is infinity—the very antithesis of straight and narrow doctrines. The sages of all cultures have always known: spiritual enlightenment is a journey of discovery rather than a fixed doctrinal destination.

Building on Abraham Maslow's influential Hierarchy of Human Needs, the psychologist Clare Graves created a model of the eight "waves" of human spirituality. "Each successive stage, wave, or level of existence is a state through which people pass on their way to other states of being." Graves believed that "man's nature is not a set thing, that it is **ever emergent**, that it is an **open system**, not a closed system"—in other words, not orthodox. Graves has had a profound influence on the cutting-edge work of Ken Wilber, Chris Cowan, Don Beck, Dudley Lynch, Paul Kordis and Dave Robinson, among others.

The waves deepen your understanding of what John the Baptist meant by "repentance." In Greek, μετανοίας means literally to turn your thinking to a different direction. Repentance does not mean turning from one narrow way to the next. It does not mean, "I once was blind, but now I am a bigot." Repentance is a continuous wave, a continuous turning, a **continuous transformation of self**. The waves are the

New wine and New

wineskins of which Jesus spoke.

http://www.peek.infinity **Mark 2: 22**

"*Development is not a linear ladder but a fluid and flowing affair, with spirals, swirls, streams and waves.*"
Ken Wilber

GROW **LEAP**

"No single decision you ever made has led in a straight line to where you find yourself now," says Deepak Chopra. Indeed, nothing in life is straight and narrow. God the Verb is always **inviting you** to catch the waves—sometimes wild, awe-inspiring waves. Yet many people complain to God, "How come I can't follow the straight path? How come I keep hitting the waves?" God's deeper message to you is this: "Don't expect a straight and narrow path in this life. Waves are a **blessing**. Waves are what prod you to grow, evolve, transform, and **leap** to the next level."

As peak performance coach Tony Robbins says, "Just when you think you have a handle on things, when things are going your way, God shows up and says, 'I want you to grow!'" The most **successful, happy** people are those who learn how to

Master the waves
—not those who avoid or deny them.

The waves can knock you out of mindlessness and open the doors to **mindfulness**—if you let them. They can transform you into a more loving, compassionate, peaceful human being— if you let them. They can **liberate** you from the bondage of your ego—if you let them. Resistance to the waves, not the waves themselves, causes suffering. The waves are always positive; your job is to **see them as positive**.

"Once we truly know that life is difficult—once we truly understand and accept it—then life is no longer difficult," writes M. Scott Peck in his classic, **The Road Less Traveled**. If there is any secret to happiness, it is in embracing the ebb and flow of life, of learning how to joyfully dance with your fears and flaws, surf with them, let the experience of riding them transform you beyond

your wildest dreams.

You reach a point, writes the philosopher Ken Wilber, when "the new wave is struggling to emerge, the old wave is struggling to hang on, and the individual feels torn, feels dissonance, feels pulled in several directions... then an opening to the next wave of consciousness—**deeper, higher, wider,** more encompassing—becomes possible."

If not for the turbulence—the frustrations, the false starts, the heartaches, the rejections, the disappointments, even the bathtub overflowing with tears—you might never discover the remarkable kingdom within you. Wild and awe-inspiring, joyous and liberating, soothing and refreshing, the waves are the canvas upon which you **paint your destiny.**

Mark 2: 23-28   http://www.dark.energy

[23]It so happened that he was walking along through the grainfields on the sabbath day, and his disciples began to strip heads of grain as they walked along.

[24]AND THE PHARISEES USED TO

ARGUE

with him: "See here, why do they do what's not permitted on the sabbath day?" [25]And he says to them: "Haven't you ever read what David did when he found it necessary, when both he and his companions were hungry? [26]He went into the house of God, when Abiathar was high priest, and ate the consecrated bread, and even gave some to his men to eat. No one is permitted to eat this bread, except the priests!" [27]And he continued: The sabbath day was created for Adam and Eve, not Adam and Eve for the sabbath day. [28]So, the son of Adam lords it even over the sabbath day.

Updates Available!

Do you believe that Christianity should be updated to meet the needs of spiritual seekers of the new millennium?

[Yes]   [No]

MIDRASH:
SPIRITUAL HUNGER

You marvel at the miracles of modern science. You watch in awe as doctors perform surgery on patients who just a few years ago had no chance of survival. It so often seems as if science is the new Christ, healing you, repairing you, even reviving you from the dead. Yet the one thing that science has not replaced is your **spiritual hunger**, your need to connect with the mystery of your own existence. Like David who hungered, you hunger.

Jesus praised David for feeding his physical hunger in a way that violated the ancient Jewish laws. Likewise, he praises you when you feed your spiritual hunger in ways that violate the ancient Christian doctrines. What Jesus said of the Sabbath, you can now say of the old religious beliefs: they were made for you, you were not made for them. The Bible was made for man, not man for the Bible. That means that **the Bible is here only to serve you** on your spiritual journey. If the old ways of interpreting its verses do not satisfy your hunger—as in the third millennium, many do not—then you are free to reinterpret them.

At one time in Jewish history, the rules of the oral and written Torah were a vibrant outgrowth of the Jews' desire to be regarded as God's "Chosen People." Rabbi Jesus came along a thousand years later, when in his view Judaism was collapsing under the weight of its rituals. Jesus' attack was never on ritual—it was on how a neglect of the heart can sterilize our rituals.

The Dalai Lama said, "If scientific analysis were conclusively to demonstrate certain claims in Buddhism to be false, then we must accept the findings of science and abandon those claims." **Jesus** most definitely would agree: if any beliefs are found to be untrue, and if these untruths prevent you from opening your heart to God, then they must be abandoned. For the Cosmic Christ, truth is measured by its

impact on your heart.

MIDRASH:

THE ANGRY JESUS

Mark frequently shows Jesus angry (3:5, 3:21, 10:14, 11:15). Later Gospel writers, such as Matthew and Luke, omit or sanitize these verses. The idea that Jesus was *"human, all too human,"* in Nietzsche's words, subject to angry outbursts just like the rest of us, did not fit into their evolving theological doctrines. One writer even described the Gospel of Mark as "Jesus Christ Raw."

Verse 5 applies to all of us, not just the Jews of the past. Jesus explains that the essential ingredient of any religion is **ethical behavior**, not ritual or doctrine. The Pharisees were not angry that this unorthodox, wavy-thinking Rabbi healed on the Sabbath; they were angry that his healing would undermine the authority of their brand of Judaism.

Although he never replaced Orthodox Judaism, Jesus did become the father of Reformed Judaism, which is essentially Christianity without Christ. Reformed Judaism is grounded in the ideas of these verses: that it is better to **do good** than bad; it is better to **save a life** than kill; and that religion should not create rules which stifle ethical behavior.

The Jesus of history never sought to replace one stifling doctrine with another or an old Bible with a new one. The early Judeo-Christian spirit can be summarized in a single phrase: **challenge the authority of doctrine**. In Jesus' day it was the Pharisees; in our day it is the fundamentalists. Even Paul—who is often misread as an apologist for fundamentalism—says that all dogma and doctrine in the world is worthless without love. "For without love we are nothing," he says. Amen.

Life   Edit   Anger   Tools   Help

 http://www.confrontation.unconscious   ▼   **Mark 3: 1-6**

¹Then he went back to the synagogue, and a fellow with a crippled hand was there. ²So they kept an eye on him, to see whether he would heal the fellow on the sabbath day, so they could denounce him. ³And he says to the fellow with the crippled hand, "Get up here in front of everybody." ⁴Then he asks them, "On the sabbath day is it permitted to do good or to do evil, to save life or to destroy it?" But they maintained their silence. ⁵And looking right at them with

ANGER EXASPERATED

at their obstinacy, he says to the fellow, "Hold out your hand!" He held it out and his hand was restored. ⁶Then the Pharisees went right out with the Herodians and hatched a plot against him, to get rid of him.

 ANGER ALERT!

Mark shows Jesus angry in verses 3:5, 3:21, 7:6, 10:14 and 11:15. Later Gospel writers omit or sanitize these verses.

Mark 3: 7-22 http://www.madness.zero.point

[7]Then Jesus withdrew with his disciples to the sea, and a huge crowd from Galilee followed. When they heard what he was doing, a huge crowd from Judea, [8]and from Jerusalem and Idumea and across the Jordan, and from around Tyre and Sidon, collected around him. [9]And he told his disciples to have a small boat ready for him on account of the crowd, so they would not mob him. ([10]After all, he had **HEALED** so **MANY** that all who had diseases were pushing forward to touch him.) [11]The unclean spirits also, whenever they faced him, would fall down before him and shout out, "You son of God, you!" [12]But he always warned them not to tell who he was. [13]Then he goes up on the mountain and summons those he wanted, and they came to him. [14]He formed a group of twelve to be his companions, and to be sent out to speak, [15]and to have authority to drive out demons. [16]And to Simon he gave the nickname Rock, [17]and to James, the son of Zebedee, and to John, his brother, he also gave a nickname, Boanerges, which means "Thunder Brothers"; [18]and Andrew and Philip and Bartholomew and Matthew and Thomas and James, the son of Alphaeus; and Thaddeus and Simon the Zealot; [19]and Judas Iscariot, who, in the end, turned him in. [20]Then he goes home, and once again a crowd gathers, so they could not even grab a bite to eat. [21]When his relatives heard about it, they came to get him.

(YOU SEE, THEY THOUGHT HE WAS
OUT OF HIS MIND.)

[22]And the scholars who had come down from Jerusalem would say, "He is under the control of Beelzebul" and "He drives out demons in the name of the head demon!"

MIDRASH:
THE SANITIZED JESUS

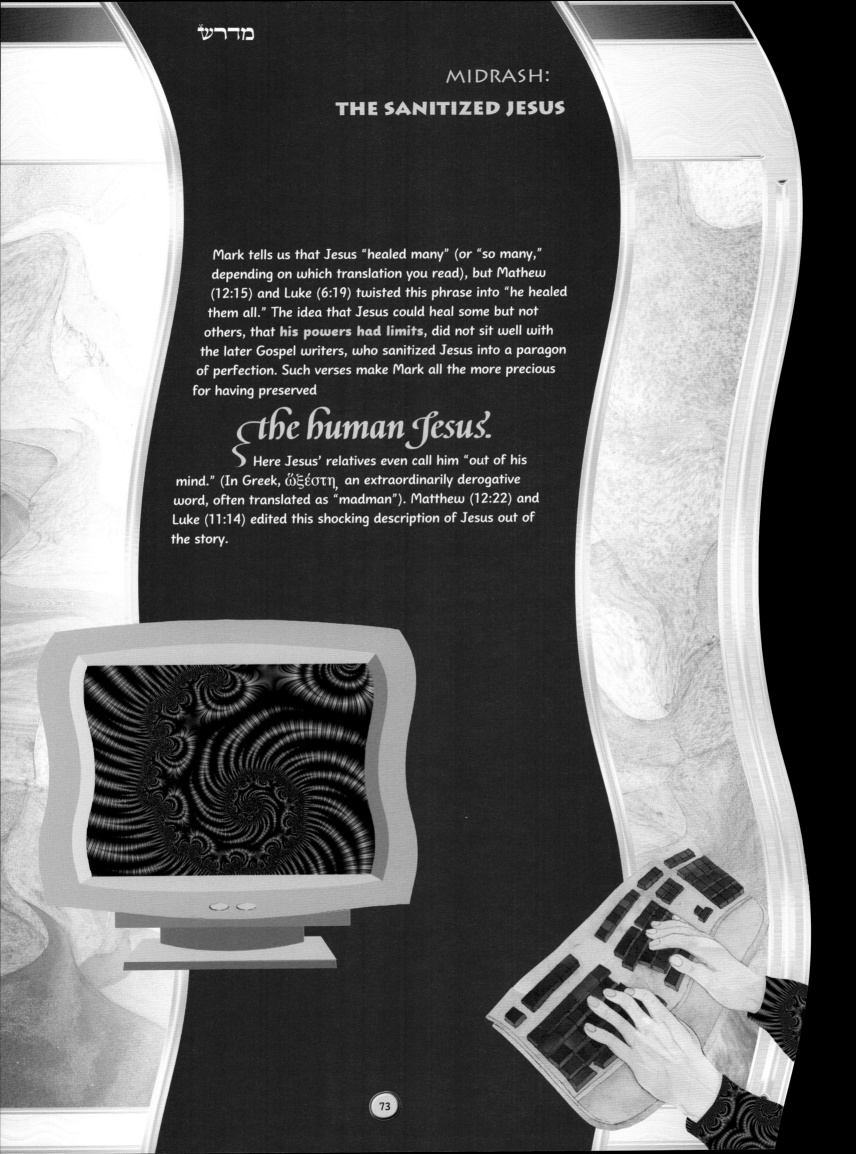

Mark tells us that Jesus "healed many" (or "so many," depending on which translation you read), but Mathew (12:15) and Luke (6:19) twisted this phrase into "he healed them all." The idea that Jesus could heal some but not others, that **his powers had limits**, did not sit well with the later Gospel writers, who sanitized Jesus into a paragon of perfection. Such verses make Mark all the more precious for having preserved

ϛthe human Jesus.

ϛ Here Jesus' relatives even call him "out of his mind." (In Greek, ὣξέστη, an extraordinarily derogative word, often translated as "madman"). Matthew (12:22) and Luke (11:14) edited this shocking description of Jesus out of the story.

MIDRASH:

QUANTUM CHRISTIANITY

"Christianity must change or die."
John Shelby Spong

Few would deny that Christianity is, in the words of Jesus, "a house divided." Thousands of respected theologians and writers recognize that current strains of Christianity suffer from too much conflict and incompatibility with our scientific age. They understand that Christianity must **reorder** and **reorganize** itself if it has any chance of surviving. They realize that Christianity has reached the bifurcation point, the proverbial fork in the road, the moment of truth when it either collapses or **spontaneously transforms** itself into a beautiful new kind of spirituality.

The doctrines and beliefs that conflict so flagrantly with the science and common sense of our day are the entropy of Christianity. They are rooted in first and second millennium dualistic thinking, which favors some and excludes others and which asserts that God is something other, something external to the *Quantum Energy* of which we are all a part.

Christianity must "escape to a higher order," to borrow a metaphor from the physicist Ilya Prigigone. Jesus never intended to create a "New Testament" (as Paul later called it) and he certainly never read it or put his stamp of approval on it. Jesus transformed the Hebrew Bible into a spectacular new faith; likewise he implores us to transform Christianity into a spectacular new faith. By his living example, Jesus taught us that the Scriptures of our great wisdom traditions are open systems—**emerging, evolving**, transformable texts, with the capacity to inspire as they change the world and to change as the world is inspired.

The last thing the historical Jesus wanted was to father a Church, and a house, divided.

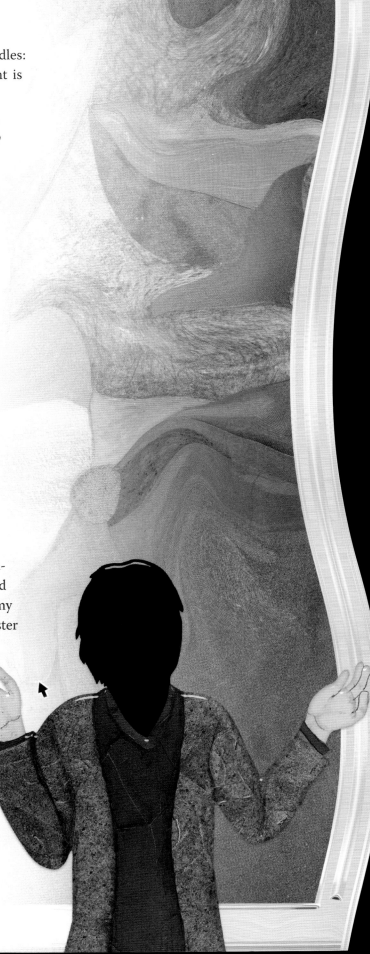

http://www.disappearance.now

Mark 3: 23-36

[23]And after calling them over, he would speak to them in riddles: "How can Satan drive out Satan? [24]After all, if a government is against itself, that government cannot endure. [25]And

IF A HOUSEHOLD IS
DIVIDED
AGAINST ITSELF, THAT HOUSEHOLD
WON'T BE ABLE TO SURVIVE.

[26]So if Satan rebels against himself and is divided, he cannot endure but is done for. [27]"No one can enter a powerful man's house to steal his belongings unless he first ties him up. Only then does he loot his house. [28]"I swear to you, all offenses and whatever blasphemies human kind might blaspheme will be forgiven them. [29]But whoever blasphemes against the holy spirit is never ever forgiven, but is guilty of an eternal sin." ([30]Remember, it was they who had started the accusation, "He is controlled by an unclean spirit.") [31]Then his mother and his brothers arrive. While still outside, they send in and ask for him. [32]A crowd was sitting around him, and they say to him, "Look, your mother and your brothers and sisters are outside looking for you." [33]In response he says to them: "My mother and brothers — who ever are they?" [34]And looking right at those seated around him in a circle, he says, "Here are my mother and my brothers. [35]Whoever does God's will, that's my brother and sister and mother!"

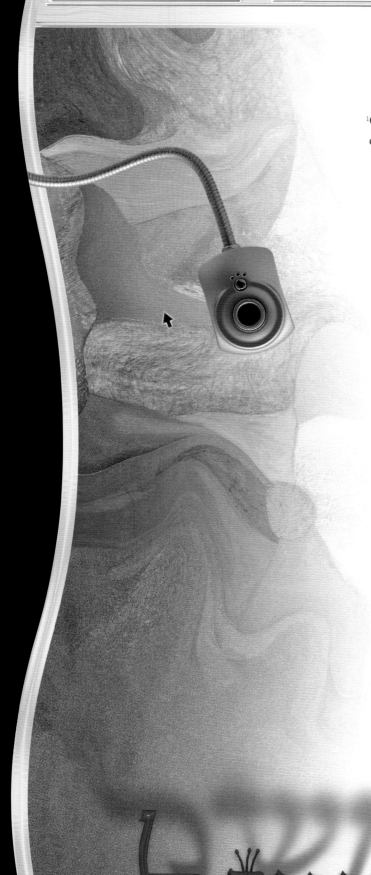

[1]Once again he started to teach beside the sea. An enormous crowd **GATHERS** around him, so he **CLIMBS** into a boat and **SITS** there on the water facing the huge crowd on the shore. [2]He would then teach them many things in parables. In the course of his teaching he would tell them: [3]Listen to this! This sower went out to sow. [4]While he was sowing, some seed fell along the path, and the birds came and ate it up. [5]Other seed fell on rocky ground where there wasn't much soil, and it came up right away because the soil had no depth. [6]But when the sun came up it was scorched, and because it had no root it withered. [7]Still other seed fell among thorns, and the thorns came up and choked it, so that it produced no fruit. [8]Finally, some seed fell on good earth and started producing fruit. The seed sprouted and grew: one part had a yield of thirty, another part sixty, and a third part one hundred. [9]And as usual he said: "Anyone here with two good ears had better listen!" [10]Whenever he went off by himself, those close to him, together with the twelve, would ask him about the parables. [11]And he would say to them: "You have been given the

SECRET

of God's imperial rule; but to those outside everything is presented in parables, [12]so that they may look with eyes wide open but never quite see, and may listen with ears attuned but never quite understand, otherwise they might turn around and find forgiveness!"

מְשָׁלִים

MIDRASH:
SECRETS

A parable is a **comparison**, something other than literal truth. A good parable shocks you out of a mental rut and catapults you to a new awareness. These Gospel stories about Jesus are themselves comparisons, references not to historical truth but to the **deeper spiritual truths** that can only be hinted at through parable and metaphor. The Hebrew word for parable is משל, the old root for shadow. Parables are shadows of divine truth that cannot be comprehended in any other way.

The key insight of Mark 4:11 is not that Jesus privately revealed anything specific or earth shattering to his disciples. Indeed, Mark rarely mentions specifics. The secret is this: do not merely sit in the meadow of life. As a mere observer, you will never reach higher levels of spirituality. You have to make a commitment and

take action...

Only then, as an active participant in the spiritual kingdom of the Cosmic Christ, will the mysteries be revealed to you. Not explicitly, but intuitively.

In Mark 4:24, Jesus teaches that everything spiritual begins within and then manifests in the physical realm. If you love, you will be loved. If you judge, you will be judged. If you damn, you will be damned. This is the Great Spiritual **Boomerang**: the vibrations you send into the Universe are the vibrations that the Universe sends back into you.

Mark 4: 13-24 http://www.eruption.mystery

[13]Then he says to them: "You don't get this parable, so how are you going to understand other parables? [14]The 'sower' is 'sowing' the message. [15]The first group are the ones 'along the path': here the message 'is sown,' but when they hear, Satan comes right along and steals the message that has been 'sown' into them. [16]The second group are the ones sown 'on rocky ground.' Whenever they listen to the message, right away they receive it happily. [17]Yet they do not have their own 'root' and so are short-lived. When distress or persecution comes because of the message, such a person becomes easily shaken right away. [18]And the third group are those sown 'among the thorns.' These are the ones who have listened to the message, [19]but the worries of the age and the seductiveness of wealth and the yearning for everything else come and 'choke' the message and they become 'fruitless.' [20]And the final group are the ones sown 'on good earth.' They are the ones who listen to the message and take it in and '**PRODUCE FRUIT**, here thirty, there sixty, and there one hundred.'" [21]And he would say to them: "Since when is the lamp brought in to be put under the bushel basket or under the bed? It's put on the lampstand, isn't it? [22]"After all, there is nothing hidden except to be brought to light, nor anything kept secret that won't be exposed. [23]"If anyone here has two good ears, use them!" [24]And he went on to say to them: "Pay attention to what you hear!

THE STANDARD **YOU** APPLY WILL BE THE STANDARD APPLIED TO **YOU**, **AND THEN SOME.**

http://www.password.trust **Mark 4: 25-34**

25"In fact, to those who have, more will be given, and from those who don't have, even what they do have will be taken away!" 26And he would say: God's imperial rule is like this: Suppose someone sows seed on the ground, 27and sleeps and rises night and day, and the seed sprouts and matures, although the sower is unaware of it. 28The earth produces fruit on its own, first a shoot, then a head, then mature grain on the head. 29But when the grain ripens, all of a sudden (that farmer) sends for the sickle, because it's harvest time. 30And he would say: To what should we compare God's imperial rule, or what parable should we use for it? 31Consider the mustard seed: When it is sown on the ground, though it is the smallest of all the seeds on the earth, 32 — yet when it is sown, it comes up, and becomes the biggest of all garden plants, and produces branches, so that the birds of the sky can nest in its shade. 33And with the help of many such parables he would speak his message to them according to their ability to comprehend. 34Yet he would not say anything to them except by way of parable, but would spell everything out in private to his own disciples.

Enter Your Password

Password hint: the one word secret to happiness

Name

Password ●●●●●

Cancel   Enter

MIDRASH:
ZEN JESUS

Mark is the only Gospel that mentions Jesus sleeping on a pillow. Even in the midst of a violent storm, he discovered a way to rest in deep peace. He taught that there is always a pillow somewhere, always something or

someone to comfort you.

So often when you hit a wave, you are tempted to lose yourself in drugs, alcohol, electronic gadgets and other material distractions. Yet you need only open your heart to the angels who everywhere surround you.

Of course, the historical Jesus did not literally stand up in the midst of a violent storm, say presto, and suddenly quiet the sea. He understood, rather, that to calm the storms of life you must first **calm the storms within** yourself. The higher levels of bliss are unknowable—only "beable."

As you ride the waves of life, sometimes up and sometimes down, you confront the deepest mystery: "The trusting mind is one with the nondual," as Sengstan, the third **Zen** patriarch, beautifully puts it. You and the waves become one.

"Seek comfort in the waves," says the Cosmic Christ. "Make a pillow of your faith."

Life   Edit   Zen   Tools   Help

  http://www.zenjesus.com   ▼   Mark 4: 35-41

[35]Later in the day, when evening had come, he says to them, "Let's go across to the other side." [36]After sending the crowd away, they took him along since he was in the boat, and other boats accompanied him. [37]Then a great squall comes up and the waves begin to pound against the boat, so that the boat suddenly began to fill up. [38]He was in the stern **SLEEPING ON A CUSHION**. And they wake him up and say to him, "Teacher, don't you care that we are going to drown?" [39]Then he got up and rebuked the wind and said to the sea, "Be quiet, shut up!" The wind then died down and there was a great calm. [40]He said to them, "Why are you so cowardly? You still don't

TRUST,

do you?" [41]And they were completely terrified and would say to one another, "Who can this fellow be, that even the wind and the sea obey him?"

[1]And they came to the other side of the sea, to the region of the Gerasenes. [2]And when he got out of the boat, suddenly a person controlled by an unclean spirit came from the tombs to accost him. [3]This man made his home in the tombs, and nobody was able to bind him, not even with a chain, [4]because, though he had often been bound with fetters and with chains, he would break the fetters and pull the chains apart, and nobody could subdue him. [5]And day and night he would howl among the tombs and across the hills and keep bruising himself on the stones. [6]And when he saw Jesus from a distance, he ran up and knelt before him [7]and, shouting at the top of his voice, he says, "What do you want with me, Jesus, you son of the most high God? For God's sake, don't torment me!" [8] — because he had been saying to it: "Come out of that fellow,

YOU **FILTHY** SPIRIT!"

[9]And (Jesus) started questioning him: "What's your name?" "My name is Legion," he says, "for there are many of us." [10]And it kept begging him over and over not to expel them from their territory. [11]Now over there by the mountain a large herd of pigs was feeding. [12]And so they bargained with him: "Send us over to the

PIGS

so we may enter them!"

MIDRASH:
THE PIGS INSIDE

If we think of each "demon" as a **negative emotion**—anger, anxiety, depression, loneliness—we can better grasp how this scene speaks to the third millennium reader. We are all a legion of emotions, many of which do not serve our Higher Selves. We often know the solution to our problems, but we resist anyway. We become so accustomed to the pigs inside that we are **afraid** of losing them, afraid of disturbing what little equilibrium we have left. The prospect of a solution torments us just as it **tormented** this man.

Many people dress nicely, live in fancy houses, and are rich and famous. But even they have moments when it feels like little pigs are running around inside of them. Often the best way to heal is to forget our pains and to help others heal theirs. Because we have felt **lonely**, we can console the lonely. Because we have been **depressed**, we can minister to the depressed. Because we have suffered, we can help the suffering.

Suffering is the
mother of compassion,
the undercurrent
of God's sea.

Healing takes courage. You have to open your heart and allow yourself to feel the pain. You have to face the little pigs inside, and sometimes even throw them off the cliff, as Jesus does in the next spread.

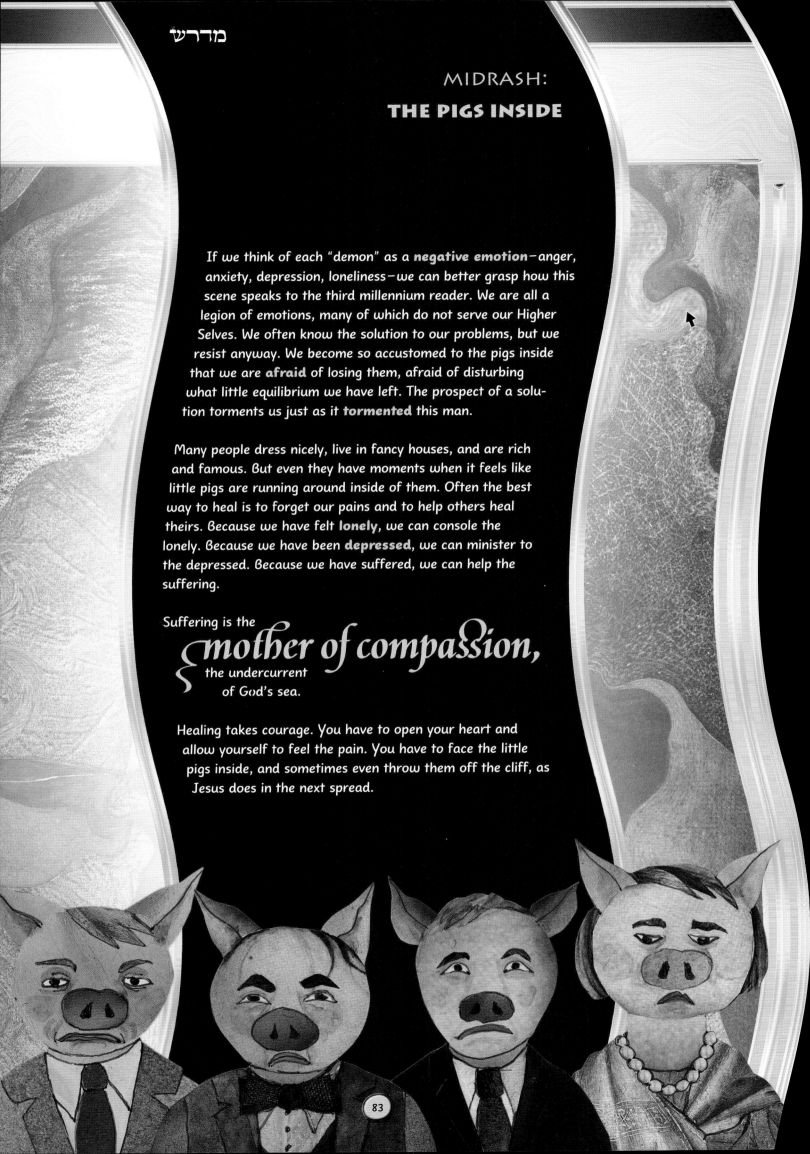

MIDRASH:
THE GRAMMAR OF GOD

The Scholars Version beautifully captures the **rhythms** of Mark's staccato, piston-driven grammar. His original Greek narrative often sounds like a piano sonata by the great Russian composer Sergei Prokoffiev. Mark was **awed** was by the story of Jesus, and eager tell it. Many modern translations mistakenly edit out the "ands." Since the days of Augustine, Mark's literary style was ridiculed as "primitive," "sloppy" and even "in poor taste." Only in the past few generations have scholars come to realize that the grammar is the engine, the momentum, the "subatomic tango" of Mark. If you read carefully, you will discover the

Ecstasy of God

in the rhythms of Mark's grammar.

Life   Edit   Tango   Tools   Help

http://www.subatomic.tango Mark 5: 13-20

[13]**AND** he agreed. **AND** then the unclean spirits came out **AND** entered the pigs, **AND** the herd rushed down the bluff into the sea, about two thousand of them, **AND** drowned in the sea. [14]**AND** the herdsmen ran off **AND** reported it in town **AND** out in the country. **AND** they went out to see what had happened. [15]**AND** they come to Jesus **AND** notice the demoniac sitting with his clothes on **AND** with his wits about him, the one who had harbored Legion, **AND** they got scared. [16]**AND** those who had seen told them what had happened to the demoniac, **AND** all about the pigs. [17]**AND** they started begging him to go away from their region. [18]**AND** as (Jesus) was getting into the boat, the ex-demoniac kept pleading with him to let him go along. [19]**AND** he would not let him, but says to him, "Go home to your people **AND** tell them what your patron has done for you — how he has shown mercy to you." [20]**AND** he went away **AND** started spreading the news in the Decapolis about what Jesus had done for him, **AND** everybody would

MARVEL.

Life   Edit   Touch   Tools   Help

Mark 5: 21-34   http://www.healingpower.touch   ▼

[21]When Jesus had again crossed over to the other side, a large crowd gathered around him, and he was beside the sea. [22]And one of the synagogue officials comes, Jairus by name, and as soon as he sees him, he falls at his feet [23]and pleads with him and begs, "My little daughter is on the verge of death, so come and put your hands on her so she may be cured and live!" [24]And (Jesus) set out with him. And a large crowd started following and shoving against him. [25]And there was a woman who had had a vaginal flow for twelve years, [26]who had suffered much under many doctors, and who had spent everything she had, but hadn't been helped at all, but instead had gotten worse. [27]When (this woman) heard about Jesus, she came up from behind in the crowd and touched his cloak. ([28]No doubt she had been figuring, "If I could just

TOUCH

his clothes, I'll be cured!") [29]And the vaginal flow stopped instantly, and she sensed in her body that she was **CURED** of her illness. [30]And suddenly, because Jesus realized that power had drained out of him, he turned around and started asking the crowd, "Who touched my clothes?" [31]And his disciples said to him, "You see the crowd jostling you around and you're asking, 'Who touched me?'" [32]And he started looking around to see who had done this. [33]Although the woman got scared and started trembling — she realized what she had done — she came and fell down before him and told him the whole truth. [34]He said to her, "Daughter, your trust has cured you. Go in peace, and farewell to your illness."

MIDRASH:

DEEP TOUCH

"The kingdom rests on the way in which we choose to touch each other and the world."

Lisa Isherwood

The vast majority of commentaries on Mark are written by men. They invariably claim that his Gospel is about persecution, suffering, crucifixion and death. They rarely share with you the real Good News in Mark:

the healing power
of a touch.

Mark uses the word "touch" eleven times—more than crucify (nine times), risen (two times) or resurrection (two times). He implores you to **touch**, not crucify. Touch, not suffer. Touch, not persecute. The Word is made flesh when you touch. You heal and become healed when you touch. But not only in the literal sense: to touch someone is to reach out with **your heart**. This is deep touch, the touch that can transform a life forever.

The nameless women of Mark have something beautiful to teach Jesus, something they could only teach him through the touch. We so often think of Jesus as the great teacher, but several of the **greatest teachers** of the Gospels are **women**. Some are named, most are nameless. They help Jesus achieve his own transformation from a wandering, rebellious Rabbi to the Anointed One (in Greek: the Christ) by touching him. In their gentle touches, these women teach a timeless lesson about Christian spirituality: it goes both ways. The Cosmic Christ anoints you but you likewise anoint the Cosmic Christ by accepting this Divine Energy into your heart. If the women had not touched him, had not overcome his mortal resistance with the authority, the exousia of the **female body**, there might never have been a Gospel of Mark or indeed the birth of a new religion. Christianity began with a simple, loving touch.

"Do not touch me " is one of the most famous lines he ever uttered, to a heartbroken Mary Magdalene (John 20:18). These simple words have inspired some of the greatest art in western history, including Tiziano's painting below and part of the Sistine Chapel, at right. Michelangelo was fascinated far more by the touch—the sensuous touch,

the naked touch,

flesh on flesh—than by the crucifixion. As Michelangelo well understood, the mysteries of creation are in the touch. Nothing **begins**, nothing is **created**, without a touch.*

Why did Jesus tell Mary not to touch him? Why does this mythical encounter between two archetypes resonate so well for third millennium readers? Because if Mary tried to touch him physically, she would have been disappointed. Jesus was no longer there in the physical sense; he was now the archetype of a new kind of Energy and a new kind of relationship to the Cosmos. he told Mary, as he now tells us: you must learn to **touch me spiritually**. Now bless everyone in your world with a loving touch."

*Sadly, even in this age of enlightenment, some people still object to seeing Michelangelo's masterpiece here, because "it shows a penis and this is a volume of the Bible." They seem not to realize that the Pope is chosen in the room where this image has graced the ceiling for 500 years. They have not made peace with their God-given bodies and seek to force their repressions and anxieties onto others. Thank God for the brave men and women of previous generations who helped to create a climate of openness, maturity and comfort about the human body.

"The body, far from being seen as sinful flesh and the site of evil has emerged as a place of revelation and moral imperatives," writes Lisa Isherwood. "Unless we are fully in our bodies we will never be able to fully *explore our divinity.*"

Life   Edit   Trust   Tools   Help

Mark 5: 35-42   http://www.fear.cure

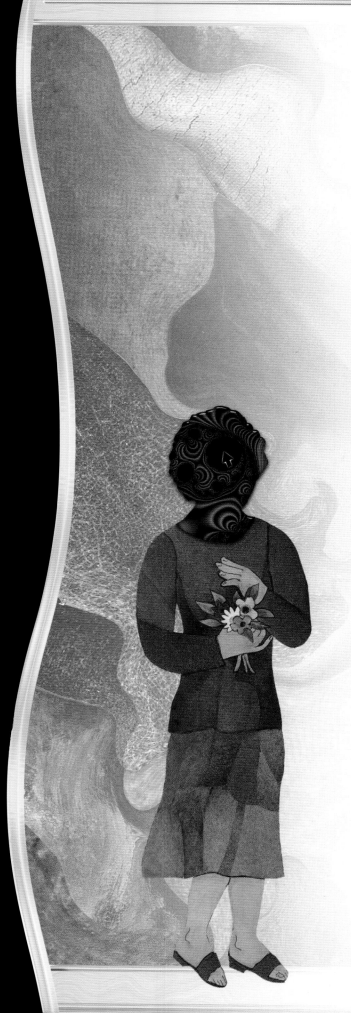

[35]While he was still speaking, the synagogue official's people approach and say, "Your daughter has died; why keep bothering the teacher?" [36]When Jesus overheard this conversation, he says to the synagogue official, "Don't be afraid, just have

TRUST!"

[37]And he wouldn't let anyone follow along with him except Peter and James and John, James' brother. [38]When they come to the house of the synagogue official, he notices a lot of clamor and people crying and wailing, [39]and he goes in and says to them, "Why are you carrying on like this?

THE CHILD HASN'T DIED; SHE'S **SLEEPING.**"

[40]And they started laughing at him. But he runs everyone out and takes the child's father and her mother and his companions and goes in where the child is. [41]And he takes the child by the hand and says to her, "talitha koum" (which means, "Little girl," I say to you, "Get up!"). [42]And the little girl got right up and started walking around. (Incidentally, she was twelve years old.)

מדרש

Mark explains, quite reasonably, that the child was not really dead but sleeping. There is a deep spiritual lesson here, which a literal reading causes you to miss: the waves of life are often not nearly as bad as they may seem. Jesus comes not to raise the child from the dead but to alert the women to their **overreaction**, to show them that the reality did not correspond to their beliefs. A key role that Jesus played in Mark was to make people aware that their

fears are just fears

and that through a single act of trust they can overcome them.

Here the lesson is: never write your own epitaph. You may think your prospects are dead, but never give up! The Cosmic Christ whispers into your ears, "Everyone else on earth may have given up on you for dead, but I trust in you. So keep going." The greatest miracle that the historical Jesus ever performed was not to raise anyone from the dead, but to **see life in people** where others failed to see it.

Mark Twain once said, "I've lived a long life and had many troubles, most of which never happened." Likewise, the wailing women in Mark 5:38 were paralyzed not by the waves but by their fear of them. Jesus' power lay in exorcising people of their fears and teaching them to trust—an entirely believable, yet miraculous skill.

Life   Edit   Ecstasy   Tools   Help

Mark 5: 42-43; 6:1   http://www.ecstasy.god   ▼

AND they were downright

ECSTATIC.

[43]**AND** he gave them strict orders that no one should learn about this, **AND** he told them to give her something to eat. [1]Then he left that place, **AND** he comes to his hometown, **AND** his disciples follow him.

MIDRASH:

ECSTASY

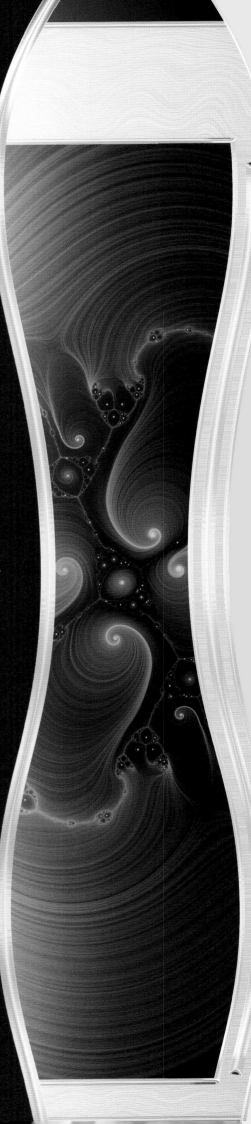

Mark uses words such as ecstasy, marvel, wonder, dumb-found and amaze 32 times, more than any other book of the New Testament. In Mark, the crowds just marvel at the Rabbi from Nazareth—they are literally ecstatic (in Greek, ἔκστασις) about what they see. If you read Mark seriously, you cannot close the book with an ounce of strength left. You slump into your chair, breathless and exhausted.

Yet as "amazed," and "ecstatic" as the crowds were by Jesus' teachings, Mark rarely tells us what these teachings were. For Mark, it was more important to report on the **ecstasy** and **wonder** that the Cosmic Christ evokes. In many respects, the **ecstasy**—not the words—is the

Quintessential message

of Mark. The miracle scenes are mere backdrops for stimulating **wonder** in the crowd, mere excuses to experience the **ecstasy** of God. You find God not by learning what to believe but by having an awe-inspiring encounter.

Mark revealed what the great theologian Rudolf Otto called the mysterium tremendum, the "blank wonder, an astonishment that strikes us dumb, amazement absolute." Sometimes it devastates us, leaving us awestruck and exhausted, while at other times, says Otto, it "comes sweeping like a gentle tide, pervading the mind with a tranquil mood of deepest worship."

In his classic book, On the Sublime, the great Greek rhetorician, known to us only as Pseudo-Longinus, wrote that true literary genius is not the ability to persuade but to "transport the audience **outside of themselves**." Pseudo-Longinus uses the Greek word ecstasis to describe this rapturous experience. "The effect of elevated language upon an audience is not persuasion but ecstasy... Our persuasions we can usually control, but the influences of the sublime bring power and irresistible might to bear, and reign supreme over every hearer." (On the Sublime 1:4)

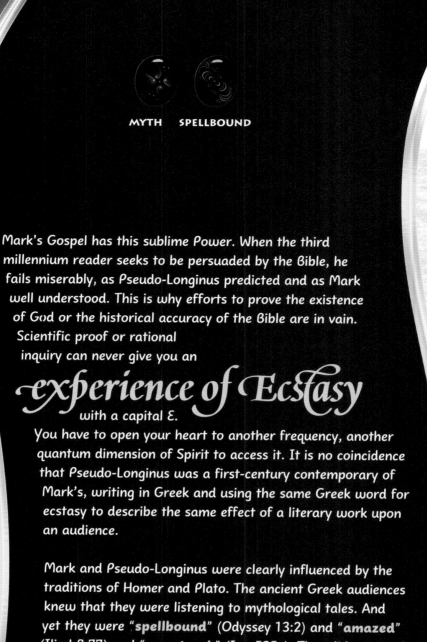

EKΣTAΣ

Mark's Gospel has this sublime Power. When the third millennium reader seeks to be persuaded by the Bible, he fails miserably, as Pseudo-Longinus predicted and as Mark well understood. This is why efforts to prove the existence of God or the historical accuracy of the Bible are in vain. Scientific proof or rational inquiry can never give you an

experience of Ecstasy

with a capital E.

You have to open your heart to another frequency, another quantum dimension of Spirit to access it. It is no coincidence that Pseudo-Longinus was a first-century contemporary of Mark's, writing in Greek and using the same Greek word for ecstasy to describe the same effect of a literary work upon an audience.

Mark and Pseudo-Longinus were clearly influenced by the traditions of Homer and Plato. The ancient Greek audiences knew that they were listening to mythological tales. And yet they were "**spellbound**" (Odyssey 13:2) and "**amazed**" (Iliad 8:77) and "**awestruck**" (Ion 535e). They did not need to believe in the myths as historical truth to experience the sublime. Why, then, are we spellbound by movies like Star Wars and the Matrix, which we know to be entirely myth, and yet not spellbound by the Gospels, which are part history and part myth? Why do Tom Clancy and Michael Crichton hold us spellbound, but not Mark and Matthew? As Erik Walker Wikstrom keenly observes, today's seekers

"turn for their spiritual sustenance to Sufi poetry, Buddhist sutras, Wiccan chants, or the mysteries of chaos theory rather than to the Bible, as if Christianity were irredeemable and all other religious traditions were pure. They are willing—even eager—to listen to the teachings of Tibetan lamas, Hindu avatars, and Mexican shaman, yet hesitant—even resistant—

to open themselves to the wisdom of the prophets or the Gospels. When it comes to Christianity, many of us have not only thrown out the baby with the bathwater, but also have tossed out the tub, shut off the lights, and walked out of the house, locking the door behind us."

Part of the reason for the exodus from the Bible among enlightened seekers is, of course, the way that certain religious leaders have poisoned its core spiritual teachings and made a mockery of one of God's greatest gifts to us—our ability to think and reason. But I believe there is a deeper reason for our defection and that the Sufi mystics and Hindu avatars were really on to something. Like the Christian mystics Hildegaard von Bingen and Meister Eckhart, the eastern sages have never needed to pop a pill to experience ecstasy. We should take them seriously precisely because they bring to the surface a critical question: is losing access to so-called "primitive" **dimensions** of ecstasy too steep a price for scientific progress?

Ask yourself: do your postmodern beliefs prevent you from enjoying our wisdom traditions? Do they prevent you from experiencing the ecstasy of God?

The 9th century Sufi mystic, Ziyad B. Al-Arabi, writes, "The beginning of ecstasy is the lifting of the veil." The veil is a reluctance to leap from ordinary awareness into a state of

exuberant allowing
which you cannot describe
or define rationally.

Mark 6: 2-3

http://www.connect.thirst

[2]When the sabbath day arrived, he started teaching in the synagogue; and many who heard him were

ASTOUNDED

and said so: "Where's he getting this?" and "What's the source of all this wisdom?" and "Who gave him the right to perform such miracles? [3]This is the carpenter, isn't it? Isn't he Mary's son? And who are his brothers, if not James, Joses, Judas, and Simon? And who are his sisters, if not our neighbors?" And they were resentful of him.

MIDRASH:
THE TEMPLE OF UNBELIEF

Mark is the only writer to note that Jesus was a τέκτων, a general handyman with carpentry and other manual labor skills. His lowly blue-collar status offended not only the High Priests of the Synagogue but also the other Gospel writers, who sought to minimize his blue-collar background. Matthew (13:55) **twisted the facts** by claiming that Jesus was "the carpenter's son"—but not a carpenter himself. In ancient times, men were almost always mentioned as sons of their fathers, not their mothers. But because Mark identifies Jesus only as "Mary's son" and never mentions Joseph, and because in the other Gospels the crowds often mock Jesus' background, many respected scholars believe that he was a ממזר, the Hebrew word for a child born of a questionable sexual union.

The people of Jesus' hometown did not believe in him, in part because he was a "mere" carpenter, likely even a bastard. Their intellectual arrogance prevented them from opening their hearts to Jesus' revolutionary message. Now we are living in a new kind of temple, a temple of Unbelief, a thoroughly rational, logical vibrational space that prevents us from diving into the mystery.

The skeptics of today are not Jews any more than they are Buddhists, Muslims, Hindus or atheists; they represent any third millennium seeker who has trouble taking Jesus seriously because he lived at the dawn of the first century and supposedly has nothing to teach us. If in our intellectual arrogance we dismiss the ideals of neighbor love and heart transformation to which Jesus gave birth, then it is we who suffer. The scholar Bruce Chilton calls them "secular Puritans" and Pastor Jim Wallis calls them "secular fundamentalists"—people who refuse to even consider the possibility that maybe there is a deeper wisdom in these Scriptures. We may live in an age of Science and Disbelief, but we still hunger for an experience of God, still

thirst to connect
to a mystery we
cannot fathom.

MIDRASH:

THE INCAPABLE JESUS

Mark is the only Gospel writer who acknowledges that Jesus was "unable to perform a single miracle." This disturbed the later Gospel writers, who twisted the phrase into "not many miracles" (Matthew 13:57). The idea that there was a time when the "son of God" was not able to perform miracles did not sit well with those who later formed the Christian canon. Yet even as an early first century writer, Mark was already steering us away from such a view. We find the secret in verses 5 and 6. Jesus could not perform miracles independent of his followers trusting that he could. Likewise, if your third millennium perspective does not permit you to trust in the Cosmic Powers in some credible way, then indeed you will never experience any miracles in your life. This is the ultimate postmodern paradox: you may resist trusting in miracles, yet when you do, they often happen.

Throughout the Gospel of Mark, the disciples and the crowds are astonished, even shocked, by Jesus. Here Jesus himself is shocked. He offers a unique gift, a powerful way of experiencing God, and what do most people do? They dismiss him.

Mark has beautifully captured a timeless truth about God and spirituality: your capacity to trust plays a critical role in everything that happens to you. The trust factor is so powerful, Mark is saying, that it can stop you from appreciating the miracles that manifest daily in your life. As the Hindu sage Yogananda says, "No one can heal us except through the cooperation of the

Hidden power
of our own thoughts."

http://www.experience.unreal **Mark 6: 4-13**

[4]Jesus used to tell them: "No prophet goes without respect, except on his home turf and among his relatives and at home!" [5]He was

UNABLE

TO PERFORM A SINGLE MIRACLE

there except that he did cure a few by laying hands on them, [6]though he was always

SHOCKED AT THEIR **LACK** OF **TRUST.**

And he used to go around the villages, teaching in a circuit. [7]Then he summoned the twelve and started sending them out in pairs and giving them authority over unclean spirits. [8]And he instructed them not to take anything on the road, except a staff: no bread, no knapsack, no spending money, [9]but to wear sandals, and to wear no more than one shirt. [10]And he went on to say to them: "Wherever you enter someone's house, stay there until you leave town. [11]And whatever place does not welcome you or listen to you, get out of there and shake the dust off your feet in witness against them." [12]So they set out and announced that people should turn their lives around, [13]and they often drove out demons, and they anointed many sick people with oil and healed (them).

WARNING! ☒

⚠ Not everyone will believe in you.

Life   Edit   Trust   Tools   Help

Mark 6: 14-238   http://www.energy.dark   ▼

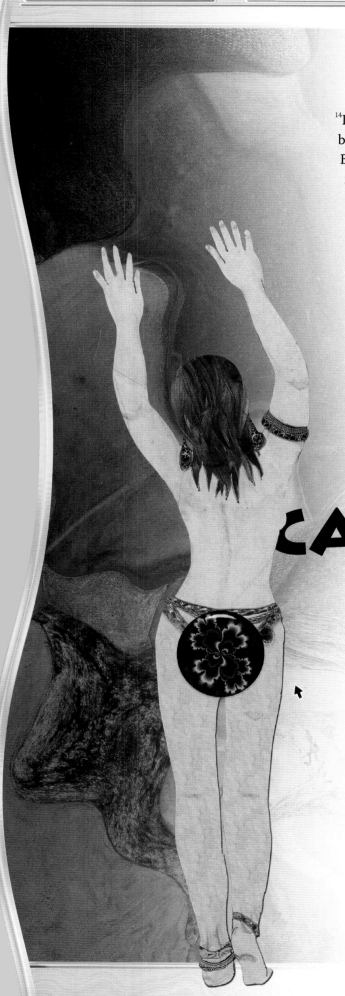

[14]King Herod heard about it — by now, (Jesus') reputation had become well known — and people kept saying that John the Baptizer had been raised from the dead and that, as a consequence, miraculous powers were at work in him. [15]Some spread the rumor that he was Elijah, while others reported that he was a prophet like one of the prophets. [16]When Herod got wind of it, he started declaring, "John, the one I beheaded, has been raised!" [17]Earlier Herod himself had sent someone to arrest John and put him in chains in a dungeon, on account of Herodias, his brother Philip's wife, because he had married her. [18]You see, John had said to Herod, "It is not right for you to have your brother's wife!" [19]So Herodias nursed a grudge against him and wanted to eliminate him, but she couldn't manage it, [20]because Herod was afraid of John. He knew that he was an upright and holy man, and so protected him, and, although he listened to him frequently, he was very confused, yet he listened to him eagerly. [21]Now a festival day came, when Herod gave a banquet on his birthday for his courtiers, and his commanders, and the leading citizens of Galilee. [22]And the daughter of Herodias came in and

CAPTIVATED

Herod and his dinner guests by dancing. The king said to the girl, "Ask me for whatever you wish and I'll grant it to you!"

[23]THEN HE SWORE AN **OATH** TO HER:

"I'll grant you whatever you ask for, up to half my domain!"

Making beautiful books

is more than just a pretty exercise. Our books mirror the spiritual health of our age. The generation of my grandparents spoke ceaselessly of their own tragedies—the Holocaust, the Second World War, the Depression. And for a while I believed them, that times were once terrible, but no more. I truly believed that life had changed since Dickens, that it was the best of times and the best of times only. Who could say, with a booming economy and a nation at peace, that there was ever a better time to be a young American than in the 1990s? Now, after 9/11, I still think it is the **best of times**, only it is the **worst of times, too.** Life is no better, only different.

That my generation witnessed 9/11 seems clear proof that we are no better, no less terrible, than those who lived before us. And that I myself witnessed such a moment still seems more than I can bear. I did not experience the event on CNN. My school building was a mile from Ground Zero. I stood on the street, in **shock** and **disbelief**, and watched the plumes of smoke billow from the towers. And then when I started running, I breathed into my lungs the particles of dead flesh.

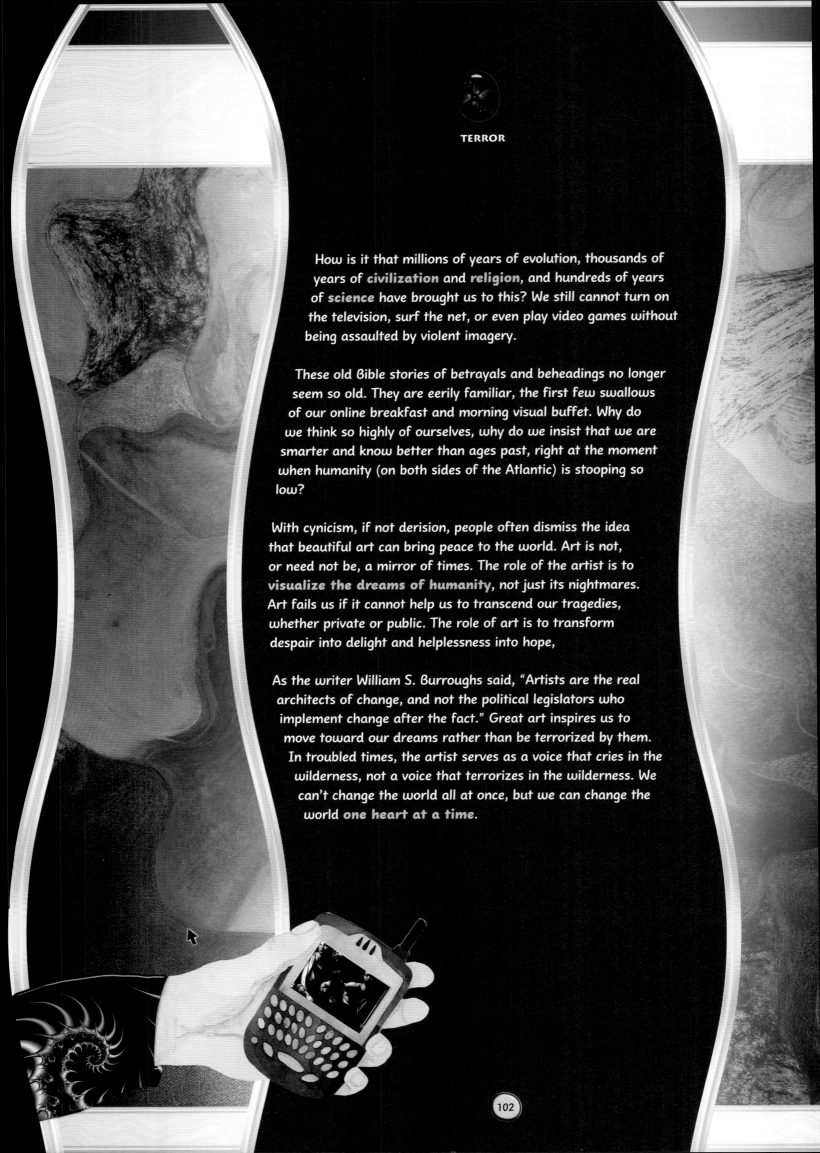

How is it that millions of years of evolution, thousands of years of **civilization** and **religion**, and hundreds of years of **science** have brought us to this? We still cannot turn on the television, surf the net, or even play video games without being assaulted by violent imagery.

These old Bible stories of betrayals and beheadings no longer seem so old. They are eerily familiar, the first few swallows of our online breakfast and morning visual buffet. Why do we think so highly of ourselves, why do we insist that we are smarter and know better than ages past, right at the moment when humanity (on both sides of the Atlantic) is stooping so low?

With cynicism, if not derision, people often dismiss the idea that beautiful art can bring peace to the world. Art is not, or need not be, a mirror of times. The role of the artist is to **visualize the dreams of humanity**, not just its nightmares. Art fails us if it cannot help us to transcend our tragedies, whether private or public. The role of art is to transform despair into delight and helplessness into hope,

As the writer William S. Burroughs said, "Artists are the real architects of change, and not the political legislators who implement change after the fact." Great art inspires us to move toward our dreams rather than be terrorized by them. In troubled times, the artist serves as a voice that cries in the wilderness, not a voice that terrorizes in the wilderness. We can't change the world all at once, but we can change the world **one heart at a time.**

http://www.humanity.dreams

Mark 6: 24-34

[24]She went out and said to her mother, "What should I ask for?" And she replied, "The head of John the Baptizer!" [25]She promptly hastened back and made her request: "I want you to give me the head of John the Baptizer on a platter, right now!" 26The king grew regretful, but, on account of his oaths and the dinner guests, he didn't want to refuse her. [27]So right away the king sent for the executioner and commanded him to bring his head. And he went away and

BEHEADED

(John) in prison. [28]He brought his head on a platter and presented it to the girl, and the girl gave it to her mother. [29]When his disciples heard about it, they came and got his body and put it in a tomb. [30]Then the apostles regroup around Jesus and they reported to him everything that they had done and taught. [31]And he says to them, "You come privately to an isolated place and rest a little." (Remember, many were coming and going and they didn't even have a chance to eat.) [32]So they went away in the boat privately to an isolated place. [33]But many noticed them leaving and figured it out and raced there on foot from all the towns and got there ahead of them. [34]When he came ashore, he saw a huge crowd and was moved by them, because they 'resembled sheep without a shepherd,' and he started teaching them at length.

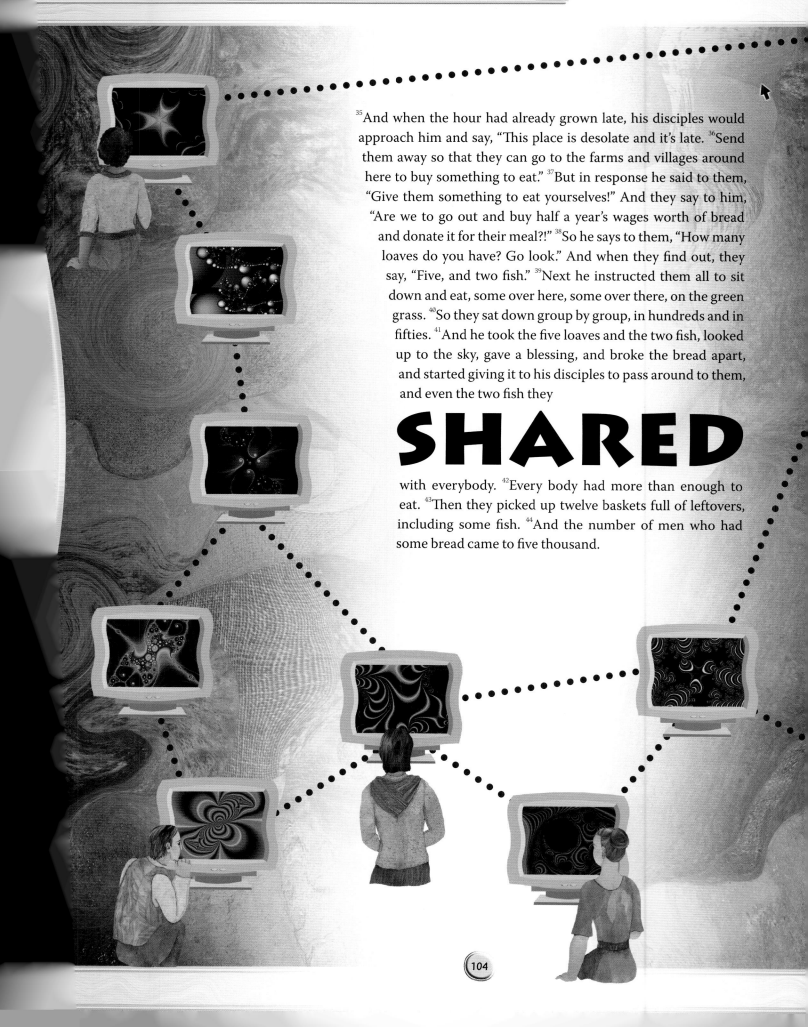

Mark 6: 35-44   http://www.wavelength.share

[35]And when the hour had already grown late, his disciples would approach him and say, "This place is desolate and it's late. [36]Send them away so that they can go to the farms and villages around here to buy something to eat." [37]But in response he said to them, "Give them something to eat yourselves!" And they say to him, "Are we to go out and buy half a year's wages worth of bread and donate it for their meal?!" [38]So he says to them, "How many loaves do you have? Go look." And when they find out, they say, "Five, and two fish." [39]Next he instructed them all to sit down and eat, some over here, some over there, on the green grass. [40]So they sat down group by group, in hundreds and in fifties. [41]And he took the five loaves and the two fish, looked up to the sky, gave a blessing, and broke the bread apart, and started giving it to his disciples to pass around to them, and even the two fish they

SHARED

with everybody. [42]Every body had more than enough to eat. [43]Then they picked up twelve baskets full of leftovers, including some fish. [44]And the number of men who had some bread came to five thousand.

MIDRASH:
SURVIVAL OF THE KINDEST

Like the disciples, we too often complain about what we lack; but the Cosmic Christ focuses us on what we have. Every leading personal development teacher of the past fifty years—including Napoleon Hill, Norman Vincent Peale, Earl Nightingale, Tony Robbins, Jim Rohn, Steven Covey, Wayne Dyer, Dennis Waitley, Bob Proctor, John Assaraf, Jeff Gitomer, Mark Victor Hansen, Deepak Chopra and Jack Canfield—has drawn on this great teaching. Begin your day with an *Attitude of Gratitude* for what you have. Learn to **be satisfied** with less, at least for now. Never focus on what you lack, but what you seek. Fill yourself with the spirit of abundance and your life will be abundant.

The Cosmic Christ may not be able to literally multiply loaves and fishes, but he can **multiply how much joy** you find in the loaves and fishes that you do have. In the truest sense, the Cosmic Christ is a multiplier—of love, compassion, tolerance and gratitude.

In other passages, Mark notes how the disciples fought among themselves (9:16, 10:35). So if there had been any struggle for food here, Mark likely would have said so. That there was no such struggle among thousands of hungry people is a testament to Jesus' ability to foster cooperation, even in difficult times. That Jesus took the time to minister to all—regardless of whether they believed in him—speaks volumes about his character. Jesus taught survival of the kindest, a teaching desperately needed today—and far more resonant than "survival of the fittest."

MIDRASH:

WISPS OF POETRY

"The miracle is not to walk on water. The miracle is to walk on the green earth in the present moment."
Thich Nhat Hanh

Here Mark borrows from the Jewish mythology of Job, especially verse 9:8, "He treads on the waves of the sea." The walking on water image is a beautiful **wisp of poetry**, certainly not literal truth, so what is its deeper meaning?

In the ever ancient, ever new writings of Augustine, we find a magnificent answer: "He comes treading the waves, keeping all the swellings and sorrows of life under his feet." Even the great Saint Augustine interpreted this scene metaphorically! Even a Church Father, writing in the early part of the first millennium, understood Mark 6:48 as a **metaphor** for the need to put the sorrows of life under our feet.

Many early Christians interpreted the Gospels much like an enlightened reader of the third millennium. They found deep resonance in the *Mysteries behind* the metaphors. They would have been puzzled, if not downright shocked, by a literal reading of Scripture.

During dokusan with a famous Zen Master, I asked why the fundamentalists have so much difficulty with metaphorical readings of Scripture. "One word," he said. "Fear. They fear what they cannot understand. They fear the **Incomprehensible**." There was compassion, not derision, in his voice. The same kind of compassion that Jesus had when he told the disciples, "Don't be afraid."

http://www.cosmic.wave

Mark 6: 45-56

⁴⁵And **RIGHT AWAY** he made his disciples embark in the boat and go ahead to the opposite shore toward Bethsaida, while he himself dispersed the crowd. ⁴⁶And once he got away from them, he went off to the mountain to pray. ⁴⁷When evening came, the boat was in the middle of the sea, and he was alone on the land. ⁴⁸When he saw they were having a rough time making headway, because the wind was against them, at about three o'clock in the morning he comes toward them walking on the sea and intending to go past them. ⁴⁹But when they saw him walking on the sea, they thought he was a ghost and they cried out. ⁵⁰By now they all saw him and were terrified. But right away he spoke with them and says to them,

"TAKE HEART, IT'S ME! DON'T BE

AFRAID."

⁵¹And he climbed into the boat with them, and the wind died down. By this time they were completely dumbfounded. (⁵²You see, they hadn't understood about the loaves; they were being obstinate.) ⁵³Once they had crossed over to land, they landed at Gennesaret and dropped anchor. ⁵⁴As soon as they had gotten out of the boat, people recognized him **RIGHT AWAY**, ⁵⁵and they ran around over the whole area and started bringing those who were ill on mats to wherever he was rumored to be. ⁵⁶And wherever he would go, into villages, or towns, or onto farms, they would lay out the sick in the marketplaces and beg him to let them touch the fringe of his cloak. And all those who managed to touch it were **CURED**!

MIDRASH:
THE PHARISEES AMONG US

We misread this section if we think that Rabbi Jesus was angry at the Judaism of the Pharisees.* He was railing against any religious framework that

Chokes our desire to love.

Everywhere I go these days, I hear pastors and scholars and even laypeople observe that the fundamentalists of our day often behave like the Pharisees of Jesus' day. Fundamentalism prescribes which beliefs are permitted and which are not, just as the Pharisees prescribed which rituals are permitted and which are not.

When Jesus quoted Isaiah 29:13, "Those people honor me with their lips, while their hearts are far from me," he could just as easily have been referring to those in our day who zealously interpret every line of Scripture in a literal, black and white way. Jesus' words apply to people of any denomination or orientation who insist that God's love is found solely—or even primarily—through doctrine or belief.

In 2 Corinthians 7:14, Paul made the mistaken (many believe bigoted) assertion that anyone who does not believe in Jesus is "lawless." How many nonbelievers have been lawful, and how many believers lawless, since the death of Jesus Christ! The disgraced televangelists and the lawless chairmen of MCI, Enron and Adelphia publicly honored Jesus with their lips while their hearts strayed far from his teachings. They lied and stole and cheated and hurt tens of thousands of people while from their lips came words such as, "I accept Jesus Christ as my personal Lord and Savior." They avoided God's commandments like the plague until they themselves became the plagues of corporate America. How accurately Isaiah and Jesus depicted them!

[1]The Pharisees gather around him, along with some of the scholars, who had come from Jerusalem. [2]When they notice some of his disciples eating their meal with defiled hands, that is to say, without washing their hands ([3]you see, the Pharisees and the Judeans generally wouldn't think of eating without first washing their hands in a particular way always observing the tradition of the elders, [4]and they won't eat when they get back from the marketplace without washing again, and there are many other traditions they cherish, such as the washing of cups and jugs and kettles), [5]the Pharisees and the scholars start questioning him: "Why don't your disciples live up to the tradition of the elders, instead of eating bread with defiled hands?" [6]And he answered them, "How accurately Isaiah depicted

YOU PHONIES

when he wrote: This people honors me with their lips, but their heart stays far away from me. [7]Their worship of me is empty, because they

INSIST ON TEACHINGS THAT ARE

HUMAN
COMMANDMENTS.

[8]You have set aside God's commandment and hold fast to human tradition!" [9]Or he would say to them, "How expert you've become at putting aside God's commandment to establish your own tradition. [10]For instance, Moses said, 'Honor your father and your mother' and 'Those who curse their father or mother will surely die.' [11]But you say, 'If people say to their father or mother, "Whatever I might have spent to support you is korban"' (which means "consecrated to God"), [12]you no longer let those persons do anything for their father or mother. [13]So you end up invalidating God's word with your own tradition, which you then perpetuate. And you do all kinds of other things like that!"

Life   Edit   Trust   Tools   Help

Mark 7: 14-24 http://www.dimension.new

[14]Once again he summoned the crowd and would say to them: "Listen to me, all of you, and try to understand! [15]What goes into you can't defile you; what comes out of you can. [16]If anyone has two good ears, use them!" [17]When he entered a house away from the crowd, his disciples started questioning him about the riddle. [18]And he says to them: "Are you as **DIM-WITTED** as the rest? Don't you realize that nothing from outside can defile by going into a person, [19]because it doesn't get to the heart but passes into the stomach, and comes out in the outhouse?" (This is how everything we eat is purified.) [20]And he went on to say,

"IT'S WHAT COMES OUT OF A PERSON THAT DEFILES.

[21]For from out of the human heart issue wicked intentions: sexual immorality, thefts, murders, [22]adulteries, envies, wickedness, deceit, promiscuity, an evil eye, blasphemy, arrogance, lack of good sense. [23]All these evil things come from the inside out and defile the person." [24]From there he got up and went away to the regions of Tyre.

MIDRASH:
THE NEW SPIRITUAL CHEMISTS

Jim Wallis tells the (now famous) story of how one of his fellow students at the Trinity Evangelical Divinity School created a "Bible full of holes." He took scissors (this was the 1960s) and cut from an old Bible every verse related to poverty, injustice and oppression —everything Jesus and the Hebrew prophets said about how nations, rulers and individuals should treat the poor. He held the Bible up as he preached, saying: "Brothers and sisters, this is our American Bible; it is full of holes. Each one of us might as well take our Bibles, a pair of scissors, and begin cutting out all the Scriptures we pay no attention to, all the biblical texts that we just ignore." This was not a critic of religion speaking; this was a Bible-believing evangelical Christian acknowledging from the pulpit that his fellow Christians were picking and choosing only those verses of the Bible that fell within their comfort zone.

Wallis revealed a **timeless truth** about how each of us relates to our wisdom traditions: no one is capable of living up to every word. Everyone

picks and Chooses.

Our national heartache is not in the picking and choosing but in the **hypocrisy** of those who deny that they pick and choose. They loudly assert that the Bible is inerrant and that they believe every word, but then do not care for the poor, do not love their neighbor, and do not love their enemies or indeed anyone who does not agree with them.

Why not just come clean and admit that we all fall short of the glory of God, that we all selectively pick and choose verses that fit into our **spiritual comfort zone**? Why all the pretending? Why the militant assertions about the need to believe in every word of the Bible, when no one on planet Earth has ever practiced every word? Why not quote those verses that we can live up to—or at least that we aspire to live up to? Why not humbly quote verses like: "Peace be to this house" (Luke 5:5). "Be rich in good works" (1 Timothy 6:18). "Live peacefully with everyone" (Romans 12:18).

Life **Edit** Synthesize Tools Help

- Judaism
- Christianity
- Hinduism
- Buddhism
- Taoism
- Islam
- New Age
- Science

http://www.spiritualchemist.com

PICK   CHOOSE   SYNTHESIZE

For over a hundred years, white Christians cited a single verse of Scripture—"Slaves, obey your masters" (Colossians 3:22)—to justify slavery in America. They ignored the hundreds of other verses in Scripture that made clear the equality and love of God for all, for example: "There is neither Jew nor Greek, slave or free, male or female; you are all one in Christ." This verse, Galatians 3:28, was never quoted by southern white Christians during the Civil War.

As Antonio says in Shakespeare's Merchant of Venice, "The devil can cite Scripture for his purpose." This is the whole point, is it not? What is our purpose when we cite Scripture? To cause divisiveness? To put down people of other faiths? To make people angry because they feel they are being proselytized? Or to bring joy to people's hearts?

The glory of living in a free society in 2007 is that we are

Spiritual Chemists,

free to synthesize elements from each wisdom tradition with the latest scientific findings. One of the great spiritual chemists of our day is the Dalai Lama, who is encouraging dialogue not only between Christians and Buddhists, but also between Buddhist meditators and neuroscientists. Another great spiritual chemist is Madonna, who boldly mixes Hinduism, Kabbalah and Christianity in her music.

One evangelical Christian accused me of being a "kitchen cabinet Christian," suggesting that I was doing something "wrong" by quoting only those verses of the New Testament with which I resonate. I receive it not as an accusation but as a **compliment**—a wondrous, joyous, alpha-enhancing compliment—that I am a "kitchen cabinet Christian." Yes, I have a little of each religion in the cabinets of my heart. I accept some from all but none as superior.

FOCUS **FIND**

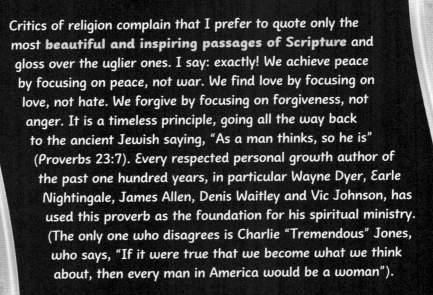

Critics of religion complain that I prefer to quote only the most **beautiful and inspiring passages of Scripture** and gloss over the uglier ones. I say: exactly! We achieve peace by focusing on peace, not war. We find love by focusing on love, not hate. We forgive by focusing on forgiveness, not anger. It is a timeless principle, going all the way back to the ancient Jewish saying, "As a man thinks, so he is" (Proverbs 23:7). Every respected personal growth author of the past one hundred years, in particular Wayne Dyer, Earle Nightingale, James Allen, Denis Waitley and Vic Johnson, has used this proverb as the foundation for his spiritual ministry. (The only one who disagrees is Charlie "Tremendous" Jones, who says, "If it were true that we become what we think about, then every man in America would be a woman").

Why should I poison my commentary with the angry verses? If you want to know the angry verses in the Bible or the Qur'an, just google "Bible angry verses" or "Qur'an angry verses." As Jesus predicts, you will find what you seek. If you seek evidence that religious people are vengeful hypocrites, you will find the evidence. Likewise, if you seek evidence of beauty and love and tolerance in all faiths, you will find that, too. **What we find is a reflection of who we are.** This is exactly what Jesus meant when he said in Mark 7:20, "It's what comes out of a person that defiles." It's the quotes that come out of us, the quotes that combust within our spiritual bloodstream that can defile us.

Jesus says, "By their fruits you shall know them." (Matthew 7:20). The verses we quote mirror the fruits within. Sadly, some evangelicals still quote 1 Corinthians 3:11, Acts 4:12, 1 Timothy 2:5, John 3:18 and 1 John 5:1. Of all the verses they could quote, they voluntarily choose to contaminate their hearts and minds with some of the most divisive, defiling verses in the Bible. (It does not serve us well to repeat them here). For every bigoted verse there are five or ten beautiful verses; life is short, time is precious, and I say: quote the beautiful ones, the inspiring ones, the ones that

bring us together.

Granted, there are times when it is necessary and constructive to advance the cause of **social justice** by quoting a negative verse. They remind us that the Bible is a fallible (however inspired) anthology of man-made books. For example, 1 Timothy 2:12 is the kind of verse that the great theologian Elizabeth Schuessler Fiorenza has quoted to **improve women's rights** around the world. But if we quote this verse in anger or to justify violent behavior it is we who are angry and violent, not the verse. Without our approbation, the verse is powerless.

Even those of a particular denomination within a particular faith pick and choose which elements to synthesize within their hearts. Many devout Catholics believe that priests should be allowed to marry and that there should be women priests —contrary to the dictates of the current Pope. Many Protestant evangelicals believe in evolution and that God is the

creative spark that triggered evolution.

Each tradition is essentially a picking and choosing, a selective synthesizing, regardless of what the most orthodox adherents claim. In fact, orthodoxy itself is a picking and choosing, a tuning out of many of the most beautiful and ecumenical passages of scripture. It is just as easy to construct a doctrine of pluralism, inclusivity and tolerance from passages of the Bible as it is to construct the opposite. That is why I spend so much time on passages such as Mark 12:34.

In later volumes of the Lost Spiritual World series (especially the Gospel of John and the letters of Paul) I often enlarge the good quotes and shrink the bad. This allows you to study Scripture in **spiritually cleansing** way. The traditional black and white text homogenizes the reading experience, forcing your eyes and your heart to give equal weight both to good and bad, positive and negative spiritual vibrations.

As I was finishing this book, I came to a profound understanding of why Biblical inerrancy is so important to some
of the fundamentalists. Inerrancy allows—Nietzsche would
say "empowers"—them to pick and choose even the most
offensive or violent verses of scripture and insist that they
represent God's will. If every verse of the Bible represents
the "infallible word of God," then any verse they cite in
defense of their political views represents the infallible word
of God. Inerrancy is a sad vacuum for verses that promote
slavery, the oppression of women, the decimation of our
environment, and the provocation of war.

One of the key insights of French philosopher Michel
Foucault is that truth claims all too often become

Power claims.

Some people quote verses that empower themselves regardless of whether they blow up in others' faces. Although Jesus
said **love your neighbor** and John and Paul said that **God
is love**, it is possible to extract verses from the Bible that
justify violence and hatred. Inerrancy gives some of the
fundamentalists an excuse not to love their enemies because
other verses imply that our enemies are the vehicles of
Satan. Inerrancy provides a tragic escape clause from God's
commandment to love—for God would never ask us to love
Satan, would he? Or so the argument goes.

In the most famous case of biblical picking and choosing,
both Protestant and Catholic authorities steadfastly refused
—until very recently—to quote from, or even read from, the
Gospel of Mark. As Brenda Deen Schildgen notes in her
landmark book, **Power and Prejudice**: The Reception of the
Gospel of Mark, "If we were to select the choice gospel in
the patristic period on the basis of the commentary tradition,
Matthew would certainly take the first place, with John a

strong second. It is noteworthy that whether Greek, Syriac or Latin, whether located in Antioch, Alexandria, Rome or Carthage, the Fathers were unanimous in their election of Matthew and John as their favorite Gospels. They were, however, almost **silent** on the Markan gospel." Schildgen reveals an astonishing statistic that shows how **picking and choosing has been an essential practice throughout Christian history.** In the third century alone, Schildgen found that Matthew was quoted approximately 11,600 times; John 4,600 times; Luke 4,000 times; and Mark only 900 times. "Mark is quoted by both the Greek and Latin Fathers about one time for every seven to ten or more of Matthew or John," she found. Church Fathers focused on those Gospels and individual verses that supported their authority and ideology, which Mark's flawed, human, even subversive Gospel did little to promote. It was canonized out of deference to the (now defunct) belief that Mark was Peter's secretary and interpreter.

The Qur'an carries the concept of selective synthesis even further. "Any verse we repeal or dismiss, we replace with a better one" (Sura 2.106). This is one of the most important spiritual concepts for the third millennium. At the very least, we can repeal the wicked verses from our hearts, if not from print. The beauty—I should say, the urgency—of our new spiritual synthesis is that we acknowledge the fallibility of our traditions, we acknowledge the good and the bad, and we choose the good. We choose 1 Corinthians 13 over Mark 13. We choose **quotes of love and quotes of peace.** We choose the emeralds and rubies and

Pearls of the Heart
—and discard the rest.

Mark 7: 24-37 http://www.jesus.curses

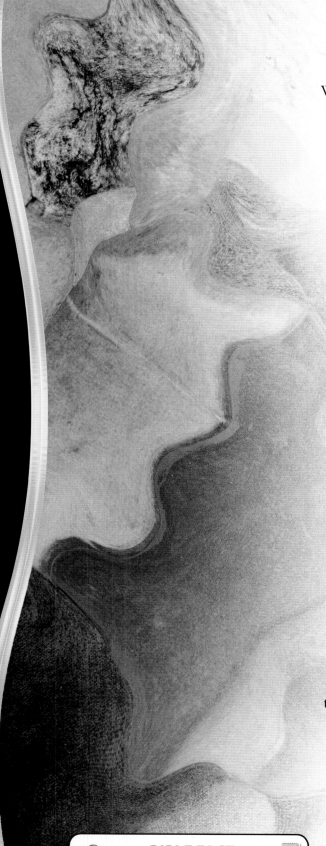

Whenever he visited a house he wanted no one to know, but he could not escape notice. [25]Instead, suddenly a woman whose daughter had an unclean spirit heard about him, and came and fell down at his feet. [26]The woman was a Greek, **BY RACE** a Phoenician from Syria. And she started asking him to drive the demon out of her daughter. [27]He responded to her like this: "Let the children be fed first, since it isn't good to take bread out of children's mouths and throw it to the

DOGS!"

[28]But as a rejoinder she says to him, "Sir, even the dogs under the table get to eat scraps (dropped by) children!" [29]Then he said to her, "For that retort, be on your way, the demon has come out of your daughter." [30]She returned home and found the child lying on the bed and the demon gone. [31]Then he left the regions of Tyre and traveled through Sidon to the Sea of Galilee, through the middle of the region known as the Decapolis. [32]And they bring him a deaf-mute and plead with him to lay his hand on him. [33]Taking him aside from the crowd in private, he stuck his fingers into the man's ears and spat and touched his tongue. [34]And looking up to the sky, he groaned and says to him, "ephphatha" (which means, "Be opened!"). [35]And his ears opened up, and right away his speech impediment was removed, and he started speaking properly. [36]Then he ordered them to tell no one. But no matter how much he enjoined them, they spread it around all the more. [37]And they were completely dumbfounded. "He's done everything and has done it quite well," they said; "He even makes the deaf hear and the mute speak!"

BIBLE FACT ☒

Jesus called the woman a κυναρίοις, which is Greek for "dog" or "bitch."

MIDRASH:
JESUS CURSES

William Barclay, the beloved Bible commentator, explains this difficult passage as follows: "The dog was not the well-loved guardian that it is today; more commonly it was a symbol of dishonor. To the Greek, the word dog meant a shameless and audacious woman; it was used exactly with the connotation that we use the word **bitch** today." Barclay believes that Jesus' use of the Greek diminutive κυναρίοις may have softened the tone, but was no less condescending.

Mark boldy captures a **prejudice in Jesus**, whose first inclination was to ignore the Gentile woman and minister only to his fellow Jews. But the woman persisted until Jesus had a change of heart. The lesson is that even Jesus had some blind spots within himself and had to grow. Mark reveals how

influential the women

were in Jesus' life and how they stimulated such remarkable spiritual growth in him—a fact whitewashed by the later Church patriarchs.

Mark tells us this story not to criticize Jesus, but to remind us that **no one is beyond spiritual growth**. We often do not grow until the spiritual wave of a stranger hits us smack in the face, purging us of our prejudices. Jesus realized that there is no such thing as clean or unclean people—a realization that became the foundation of Paul's ministry.

MIDRASH:

SPIRITUAL ABUNDANCE

Nearly all of the great artists have interpreted this scene literally, showing a banquet of thousands of loaves and fishes passed around in baskets filled to the brim. In fact, Renaissance artists idealized this scene as the "Multiplication of Loaves and Fishes." But if you focus on the historicity of this story, you miss the point entirely. In verse 42, Mark says simply that "they ate and were **satisfied**," as the New International Version (NIV), a conservative evangelical translation, puts it. He does not say that Jesus miraculously created more food. Later Gospel writers, especially John, inflated this into a miracle scene.

The key word here is "satisfied." How many times have you eaten in the best restaurants, or sat in the best seats at a show, yet still left unsatisfied? Satisfaction is a very spiritual thing. You can eat a steak and be unsatisfied by its toughness or lack of flavor, or you can eat a juicy ripe peach and feel like you are in heaven. Jesus had an unusual gift of **making people feel like they were in heaven** while here on earth, so that whatever he put before them, they were satisfied. Mark even says that there was plenty of food left over; such is the atmosphere of abundance that the Cosmic Christ (or Cosmic Source, or whatever you want to call it) can create in your life, seemingly out of nothing. Even a small morsel of bread, infused with the Spirit of your Cosmic Source, can satisfy your hunger.

How many in America—the wealthiest nation in history—go to bed unsatisfied? It is curious indeed that our incredible wealth and abundance does not seem to have made us any more fulfilled. This is the Lost Spiritual World that we seek to recover, the Holy Grail of 21st century science: how to be satisfied, how to feel that

inner abundance,
of which Mark wrote.

¹And once again during that same period, when there was a huge crowd without anything to eat, he calls the disciples aside and says to them, ²"I feel sorry for the crowd, because they have already spent three days with me and now they've run out of food. ³If I send these people home hungry, they will collapse on the road— in fact, some of them have come from quite a distance." ⁴And his disciples answered him, "How can anyone feed these people bread out here in this desolate place?" ⁵And he started asking them, "How many loaves do you have?" They replied, "Seven." ⁶Then he orders the crowd to sit down on the ground. And he took the seven loaves, gave

THANKS,

and broke them into pieces, and started giving (them) to his disciples to hand out; and they passed them around to the crowd. ⁷They also had a few small fish. When he had blessed them, he told them to hand those out as well. ⁸They had **MORE THAN ENOUGH TO EAT**. Then they picked up seven big baskets of leftover scraps. ⁹There were about four thousand people there. Then he started sending them away.

[10]And he got right into the boat with his disciples and went to the Dalmanoutha district. [11]The Pharisees came out and started to argue with him. To test him, they demanded a sign in the sky. [12]He groaned under his breath and says,

"WHY DOES THIS GENERATION INSIST ON A SIGN?

I swear to God, this generation won't get any sign!" [13]And turning his back on them, he got back in the boat and crossed over to the other side. [14]They forgot to bring any bread and had nothing with them in the boat except one loaf. [15]Then he started giving them directives: "Look," he says, "watch out for the leaven of the Pharisees and the leaven of Herod!" [16]They began looking quizzically at one another because they didn't have any bread. [17]And because he was aware of this, he says to them: "Why are you puzzling about your lack of bread? You still aren't using your heads, are you? You still haven't got the point, have you? **ARE YOU JUST DENSE?** [18]Though you have eyes, you still don't see, and though you have ears, you still don't hear! Don't you even remember [19]how many baskets full of scraps you picked up when I broke up the five loaves for the five thousand?" "Twelve," they reply to him. [20]"When I broke up the seven loaves for the four thousand, how many big baskets full of scraps did you pick up?" And they say, "Seven." [21]And he repeats, "You still don't understand, do you?"

MIDRASH:
THE GREAT REALIZATION

A long time ago, a wealthy man named Shakyamuni found himself deeply troubled by the cycle of life and death. He saw that our time on this earth is painfully short and in constant flux; everything is transitory, with nothing permanent to grasp onto. So Shakyamuni shaved his head, donned the robes of a monk and began a punishing regimen of fasting, meditating, begging for food and depriving himself of sleep. After six years he was exhausted, starved physically and mentally, a virtual skeleton beyond the recognition of family and friends. He decided to eat, sleep and nourish himself back to health. Then one day he sat under a bodhi tree, lost himself in deep meditation and achieved Enlightenment.

Shakyamuni's Great Realization was that all he was looking for was **already within him**. He realized that all that searching, all that probing of the Universe for a sign, was in vain. There are no signs, no magical answers external to us; each of us is complete, with the magnificent potential to become awakened. This man Shakyamuni gave birth to a great religion; he became "**the awakened one**"—in Sanskrit, the Buddha.

As Mark makes clear, Jesus did not need a sign and did not want you looking for a sign. Likewise the Buddha and Lao Tzu and Muhammad and the other great prophets did not need a sign. You will not find **Enlightenment** by wasting your life arguing about divisive doctrines or end-time prophecies, as if they are literal signs from a literal God who spies on you from the clouds in the sky. You find it within by

transforming your heart

and by treating others with love and respect. Your capacity to experience joy, love and peace without a sign—and without a doctrine—is what leads you to Enlightenment.

MIDRASH:
PATTERN INTERRUPTS

Only Mark tells this unusual story of Jesus spitting into the eyeballs of a blind man. Sometimes words alone do not work; you need a physical jolt. Tony Robbins often does this by unexpectedly splashing cold water into the faces of depressed people. He creates a "pattern interrupt" which gets their minds off their misery; then through laughter or other techniques, he heals them. Jesus was, likewise, a master of the **pattern interrupt**, saying or doing shocking things. When the waves get wild, when you are nervous and lonely and vulnerable, the Cosmic Christ comes right in and

Zaps you with a smile.

Life   Edit   Zap   Tools   Help

http://www.zeropoint.zap

Mark 8: 22-26

²²They come to Bethsaida, and they bring him a blind person, and plead with him to touch him. ²³He took the blind man by the hand and led him out of the village. And he

SPAT
INTO HIS EYES,

and placed his hands on him, and started questioning him: "Do you see anything?" ²⁴When his sight began to come back, the first thing he said was: "I see human figures, as though they were trees walking around." ²⁵Then he put his hands over his eyes a second time. And he opened his eyes, and his sight was restored, and he saw everything clearly. ²⁶And he sent him home, saying, "Don't bother to go back to the village!"

Mark 8: 27-30 http://www.quantum.spirit

[27]Jesus and his disciples set out for the villages of Caesarea Philippi. On the road he started questioning his disciples, asking them, "What are people saying about me?" [28]In response they said to him, "(Some say, 'You are) John the Baptist,' and others, 'Elijah,' but others, 'One of the prophets.'" [29]But he continued to press them,

"WHAT ABOUT YOU, WHO DO YOU SAY I AM?"

Peter responds to him, "You are the Anointed!" [30]And he warned them not to tell anyone about him.

MIDRASH:
YOU DECIDE

We all come to a moment of reckoning in our lives when we must decide for ourselves who the Cosmic Christ is and what he means to us. Peter and the others did not understand who Jesus was until this moment, deep into the eighth chapter. Likewise, many of us do not encounter the Cosmic Christ until we are deep into our lives, often in a middle or later chapter. We have heard of Jesus, maybe even read the Gospels as literature, but never experienced the Cosmic Christ as a **living presence**.

Jesus implored his disciples to distinguish between who others said he was and who they said he was. This is the key: do not worry about what other people say about him. The Cosmic Christ asks only, "Who do you say I am?" So Peter called him the Anointed. That was Peter; but you are not Peter and his response need not be yours. The Cosmic Christ enters your life the moment you realize that *only you can define* your relationship to him. Only you can activate the buttons inside your heart. You need not believe that Jesus was the Jewish Messiah or the supernatural son of God to appreciate his message in the deepest way. Call him a "good teacher," if you wish, as many of the first Christians did.

In the Gospel of Thomas (13), the historical Jesus clearly allowed for multiple interpretations of his mission, each according to his capacity and need. "Jesus said to his disciples, "Compare me to something and tell me what I am like." Simon Peter said to him, "You are like a just angel." Matthew said to him, "You are like a wise philosopher." Thomas said to him, "Teacher, my mouth is utterly unable to say what you are like."

http://www.ego.peel

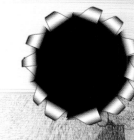

[31]He started teaching them that the son of Adam was destined to suffer a great deal, and be rejected by the elders and the ranking priests and the scholars, and be killed, and after three days rise. [32]And he would say this openly. And Peter took him aside and began to lecture him. [33]But he turned, noticed his disciples, and reprimanded Peter verbally: "Get out of my sight, you Satan, you, because you're not thinking in God's terms, but in human terms." [34]After he called the crowd together with his disciples, he said to them, "If any of you wants to come after me, you should

DENY YOURSELF,

pick up your cross, and follow me! [35]Remember, by trying to save your own life, you're going to lose it, but by losing your life for the sake of the good news, you're going to save it. [36]After all, what good does it do to acquire the whole world and pay for it with life? [37]Or, what would you give in exchange for life?

"IF YOU WANT TO BECOME FULL, LET YOURSELF BE EMPTY. IF YOU WANT TO BE REBORN, LET YOURSELF DIE."

LAO TZU

MIDRASH:
THE SECRET OF SECRETS

Many of us throw in the towel with Christianity when we hear, "Deny yourself and pick up the cross." It sounds so pessimistic and despairing—even self-loathing. But the

Hindu and Sufi mystics

offer a life-affirming perspective on this passage. Sometimes you need to step outside of a faith to appreciate it more deeply.

In Hindu philosophy, the Sanskrit word jivanmukta means "freed while living." This is one of the great purposes of the wisdom traditions—to free you from the destructive side of your ego. As the great Persian poet Rumi writes,

"If you could get rid of yourself just once, the secret of secrets would open to you."

The wisdom traditions teach you to **suspend your ego**—not because you are not worthy, not because you are a "sinner" —but because your ego **blocks your receptivity** to the deeper mysteries of Cosmic Awareness. "When you are free from self, God will show His Beauty," said the 14th century Sufi poet Mahmud Shabistari. "Be the captive of Love in order that you may be truly free—free from coldness and the worship of self," adds Abd Al-Rahman Jami, also a Sufi poet.

When I realized that "picking up the cross" is not a uniquely Christian concept—that in fact, its spiritual roots predate Christianity by at least a thousand years—I recognized it as a timeless spiritual principle, part of what Aldus Huxley called "the perennial philosophy." To "pick up the cross" does not mean "be a martyr for Christ." It does not mean you should drown in the waves of sorrow. It means: seek a better, more spiritually enriching life. **Crucify your doubts and fears**—whatever prevents you from living a joyful life. The crucifixion of self is simply the crucifixion of the self you no longer want to be.

http://www.field.ripples

[38]"Moreover, if any of you are

ASHAMED

OF ME AND MY MESSAGE

in this adulterous and sinful generation, of you the son of Adam will likewise be ashamed when he comes in his Father's glory accompanied by holy angels!" [1]And he used to tell them, "I swear to you: Some of those standing here won't ever taste death before they see God's imperial rule set in with power!"

MIDRASH:

DEEP FORGIVENESS

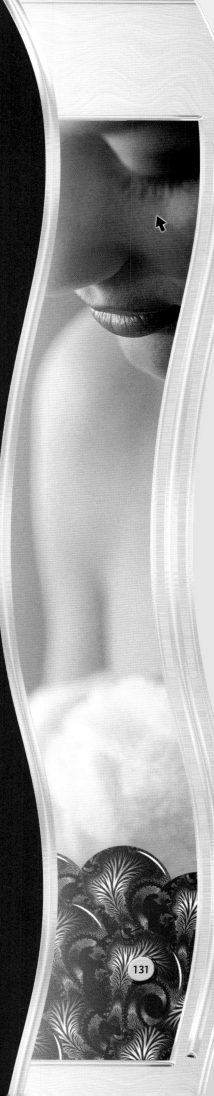

"To be forgiven, first you must forgive."
Sir John Templeton

At first, I openly shared my love for the Cosmic Christ. He had so cleansed my heart, so uplifted and inspired my soul, that I awoke every morning in a flowerbed of gratitude for being alive and for knowing his love. But when I told people of this profound yet simple message—to love your neighbor and transform your heart—they often pigeonholed me as one of those "Jesus freaks." I soon discovered how many people are offput by the vocal minority of fundamentalists and evangelicals who seek to impose their doctrines upon an unwilling public. I suddenly felt deeply ashamed at calling myself a Christian—exactly what Jesus warned against in Mark 8:38. And then, in the most painful irony of all, I met a legion of people who insisted that I am not a Christian because I do not believe what they believe.

Knowing the Cosmic Christ has nothing to do with "being saved" or "going to heaven" or trying to convert others. Knowing the Cosmic Christ is simply about having a loving heart.

The most difficult thing to do is to forgive those who do not accept you for who you are, to

tolerate the intolerant,

to include those who exclude, to acknowledge from the depths of your heart that everyone is a child of God, every bit as wonderful as you.

For me, this meant not merely tolerating the fundamentalists and evangelicals who hurt me, but finding a way to love and forgive them "with all my heart and all my soul and all my might," to borrow a phrase from the Torah (Deuteronomy 6:5).

First I allowed myself to feel the pain, the God-awful pain. I relived the feelings of rejection, desolation, alienation and loneliness. I felt the groundswell of anger at the evangelicals for their overwhelming support of the war in Iraq. I wept until my blouse was soaked, my stomach convulsed and I could barely breathe. Then I cried out for release from this inner torment. "Give me the strength to forgive!" I wailed.

Suddenly I found myself on a spiritual and emotional plane that I cannot adequately describe. I was sitting privately with Jesus, the Buddha, Hildegaard von Bingen, Georgia O'Keeffe and several among the living, whose privacy I shall respect. I asked them to look deep inside the secret chambers of my heart and verify for me that I had **genuinely forgiven** those who had hurt me. I prayed that if there were one shred of pain or anger or shame left, that they would please dig deep into my heart and purge me of that final shred. A flash flood of tears and then a pulsation of joy swept through my body. I burst into laughter—not comic laughter, but relief laughter, as my spiritual heroes probed deep into my heart and saw that it was pure.

I asked them to forgive those who had caused me such anger and shame. And immediately, without hesitation, they forgave them. How quickly and easily they forgave them!

Then the veil was lifted: I realized that the fundamentalists and evangelicals had come into my life for a reason. They were God's **invitations to heal and transform myself**, to discover that knowing God is more than simply loving those who love you. I finally understood what Dostoevski meant when he said, "Hell is when you suffer from an inability to love." I realized that forgiveness is more than polite tolerance. Forgiveness means releasing with every ounce of blood and tears any animosity you might feel— and then sending a

loving vibration

into the world.

Paul wrote, "I hope from the depths of my heart that I will not be ashamed" (Philippians 1:20). Like Paul, I was born Jewish. Like Paul, I was taught that Christianity was "no no," a religion I dare not consider. I freely admit that for most of my life I would have been ashamed to pour out my heart in a book about Jesus. Now I am honored and grateful to call myself a **Christian**, just as I am honored and grateful to call myself a **Jew** and a **Buddhist** and a **Hindu** and a **Taoist**. Every morning, I say this affirmation: "I am a child of God, ashamed of nothing, grateful for who I am."

You need not believe that the Bible is the infallible word of God or that the Pope is the infallible messenger of God. You can trust in something better—that our wisdom traditions can bring you closer, as the Bible scholar Marcus Borg says, to that "stupendous, magnificent,

wondrous More."

Yes, there is something "out there"—some Elusive Energy, some strange and magnificent Spiritual Cosmos that Jesus and the other great prophets tapped into. You need not understand it, or even name it, to be humbled by its power to transform.

In the Tao Te Ching (64a), Lao Tzu said, "A journey of a thousand miles begins beneath one's feet." It begins within the heart, too; and the first step is forgiveness.

[2]Six days later, Jesus takes Peter and James and John along and leads them off by themselves to a lofty mountain. He was

TRANSFORMED

in front of them, [3]and his clothes became an intensely brilliant white, whiter than any laundry on earth could make them. [4]Elijah appeared to them, with Moses, and they were conversing with Jesus. [5]Peter responds by saying to Jesus, "Rabbi, it's a good thing we're here. In fact, why not set up three tents, one for you, and one for Moses, and one for Elijah!" ([6]You see, he didn't know how else to respond, since they were terrified.) [7]And a cloud moved in and cast a shadow over them, and a voice came out of the cloud: "This is my favored son, listen to him!" [8]Suddenly, as they looked around, they saw no one, but were alone with Jesus. [9]And as they were walking down the mountain he instructed them not to describe what they had seen to anyone, until the son of Adam rise from the dead. [10]And they kept it to themselves, puzzling over what this could mean, this 'rising from the dead.' [11]And they started questioning him: "The scholars claim, don't they, that Elijah must come first?" [12]He would respond to them, "Of course Elijah comes first to restore everything. So, how does scripture claim that the son of Adam will suffer greatly and be the object of scorn? [13]On the other hand, I tell you that Elijah in fact has come, and they had their way with him, just as the scriptures indicate."

From Fra Angelico to Perugino to Tiziano, most artists throughout history have represented the Transformation literally, showing Moses and Elijah actually speaking with Jesus in garments white as snow. But the third millennium reader, who interprets this scene metaphorically, seeks a deeper insight into the nature of spiritual transformation. Mark brings us as close as we will ever get to that mystical moment when Jesus was transformed from an itinerant Rabbi into the archetype of a

New Spiritual Power
– the Cosmic Christ.

The crucifixion is so deeply embedded in our visual consciousness that when we see something as great—and as deceptively similar—as Fra Angelico's Transformation, we pass it by. But notice: there is no cross, no nails, no blood. The open arms symbolize the **open heart**, the **open mind**, the **newness of spirit**. This is Fra Angelico's masterpiece, his real ecce homo—not the crucifixion.

What happened on Mount Tabor is far more resonant for third millennium readers than what happened at Calvary. Even the evangelical scholar James R. Edwards confesses, "The Transformation of Jesus is a singular event in ancient literature. It has no analogy in the Bible, or in the extrabiblical literature from the Apocrypha, Pseudepigrapha, rabbinic literature, Qumran, Nag Hammadi, or in Hellenistic literature as a whole." The crucifixion and the resurrection, on the other hand, have so much analogy to other literatures that most scholars question their historicity. But the Transformation is beyond question: it makes a profound contribution to our understanding of human spirituality.

In his letters, Peter never mentions the crucifixion or the resurrection, for he was not there, having abandoned Jesus and run for his life. He offers only one proof for the claim that Jesus is the Christ, only one observation that the Gospel stories are not "cleverly invented myths." (Peter even uses the word "myth"—μύθοις in Greek). And that is the Transformation. "We ourselves heard the voice that came from heaven when we were with him on the holy mountain," he later recalled (2 Peter 1:16-19). The transformation, far more than any event in the life and ministry of Jesus, had the biggest impact on Peter and the disciples; it was the defining moment of their lives. Peter hits a rare moment of poetry when he described the emotional impact of the Transformation—it's like "when the **morning star rises in your hearts.**"

"The real transfiguration on Tabor was not the change of Christ into something he was not before, but the change of the perceptive capabilities of the apostles," writes Andreas Andreopoulos, a scholar and expert in the Transformation. **This is the secret**—the transformation is not about Jesus; it's about you. Now you are the Cosmic Seeker, now you are the one to witness the morning star rising in your heart.

It is fascinating that a prominent theologian called "pseudo-Dionysios," who lived in the sixth century, described the transformation much like a third millennium thinker: "We grasp the transformation in the best way we can, as it comes to us wrapped in the sacred veil of love." Such a beautiful phrase—

sacred veil of love!

HEAR   AWAKE   TRANSCEND

Mark imagines Jesus talking with Moses and Elijah because the greatest spiritual transformations must always involve the past in some way. Without a meaningful anchor in our past, we are **lost**. The word transform (from the Greek μετεμορφώθη (metamorphosis) means to change from one form to another. If we think of the past and present as forms, then we understand: transformation in the present involves a transformation of the past.

If we recall the opening verses of Mark (1:11), the heavens split and a voice says, "You are my Son, beloved; in you I take pleasure." Now read Mark 9:7 carefully: "This is my son, the beloved: hear him." Notice that Mark inserts the phrase "hear him" at just the moment we are ready to hear. It is as if we have not really been hearing for these past nine chapters, not yet been entirely awakened, not understood that the real "Good News" is our capacity to transform.

Mark 9:2 is the

defining moment

of the Christian Testament. The disciples came to a new awareness of who Jesus was. Are you, likewise, ready to come to a new awareness of your spiritual place in the Universe? Ready to transcend your imagined barriers and live the life that you know, deep down, you were destined to live?

"We must be **awake** now," writes Spurgeon, "for we traverse the enchanted ground."

As the great theologian Rudolf Bultmann says, "There can only be one criterion for the truth of revelation, namely, that the revelation pushes us to make a decision." It is right here, with the transformation, that we decide to give birth to new meanings, new transformations of the old Christian myths. We are all Marys, all virgins of the new millennium's spirit, gazing into deep space through the eyes of the Hubble telescope or probing deep into the mind with an MRI, wondering: what beautiful spiritual world shall be born of our dreams, what heaven on earth shall we create?

We have liberated ourselves from oppressive readings of Scripture. We no longer pander to the patriarchs. We no longer read the Bible literally. But what shall we do with our newfound freedom? Liberation is a double-edged sword. Without transformation, liberation often leads to existential despair. Our next step, says Elisabeth Schussler Fiorenza, is to transform the past, to "search the rich dark depth of submerged religious wisdom and knowledge that can inspire sacred visions for a different future."

At first, on page 135, we saw Fra Angelico's image of the transformation created in the second millennium; from now on we use an image created in the third. Before, the trans-formed was a man; now it is man and woman. Before, the transformed was the son; now

each of us is a Sun.

The transformed woman looks serenely at the men and women in her life. They are not disciples, but friends, lovers, participants in the glory that is God. Each of us has our turn at transformation—not a glorification of self but a glorification of how the self is transformed through our Sacred Source.

BIRTH   ENERGIZE   LEAP

"Each self is a **unique mirror of divinity** and therefore each person births a unique creation when he or she lets the true self be born," writes Matthew Fox. Our focus is now on how the Cosmic Christ transforms us rather than how the historical Jesus was himself transformed. When we step into the light of God, we energize ourselves. This is God—not only the energy, but also the energizing:

God the verb,
God the Transformer.

What joy! To put ourselves in the light—not the limelight, but the Godlight! As Paul writes, "For God made his light shine in our hearts" (2 Corinthians 4:6). This shining of the light in our hearts is the essence of transformation. Paul himself was transformed from a persecutor of Christians to a progenitor of Christians. From hatred to love: this was Paul's magnificent change of heart. "Be transformed by the renewing of your mind," he said (Romans 12:2).

The Gospel of Mark is not about the Jesus of history. It is about how the Energy he tapped into **leaps** from the pages of history into our hearts. Only by injecting ourselves into the story can the story live through us. The story comes alive when we declare, with Meister Eckhardt, "Here, in my own soul, the greatest of all miracles has taken place."

As Luke explains (9:32), we are asleep until the transformation. We awake when we realize the significance of the transformation—the **sudden release** of our full powers, an orgasm of spirit; a **sudden rising** to the surface of our latent powers, powers we never experienced before or could not easily harness without the help of the Cosmic Christ. Now here is that power, that new Spirit. Just as the Buddha is "the awakened one," the Christian is "the transformed one."

Now we realize: the Cosmic Christ represents an *energy field* that permeates our hearts as well as the heart of all reality. The Jesus of history tapped into this field—this was his secret—and our capacity to tap into the field with him is independent of our cultural framework, whether in first century Nazareth or third century America.

Now we realize: the miracle stories are not miracles—or even myths. They are transformations. "I once was lost, but now I am found" (Luke 15:24). "I once was blind, but now I can see" (John 9:25). I once was sick, but now I am healed. I once was hungry, but now I am satisfied. Most of the miracle stories in the Christian Testament can be reduced to this simple transformational structure: "I once was ---, but now I am ---."

When we become aware of this formulation as a kind of "**deep structure**," a recurring theme and spiritual undercurrent of the entire Christian Testament, our understanding of Christianity is transformed. The Gospel stories are transformation stories. We might even call the Gospel of Mark the Transformations of Mark.

The fundamentalists are right about this: the Bible still has exousia, still has authority in the third millennium. Through its unique assimilation of history, poetry and myth, the Bible still has the power to transform. The kingdom of God is the coming to **a new awareness of the power** of transcendence. As Gandhi once said, God "is proved not by extraneous evidence but in the transformed conduct and character of those who have felt the real presence of God within."

The Treatise on the Resurrection, one of the lost Christian manuscripts rediscovered at Nag Hammadi, offers a profound definition of the resurrection: "It is the revelation of what is, the transformation of things, and a transition into newness" (48:34-38). Many of the early Christians understood that the resurrection **happens to us now**, in the form of spiritual transformation—not in any "life to come."

The measure of the spiritual genius of a culture is its capacity to transform. The deeper the existential or postmodern despair, the greater the possible transformation. Our third millennium crisis of faith is poised to yield an even greater faith. Transformation is the greatest life affirming principle. We transform the ugly **into** the beautiful, the mean **into** the kind, depression **into** joy, sadness **into** happiness, tears **into** laughter, even war **into** peace. All negatives exist for the pure joy of transforming them **into positives**. All evil exists for us to transform **into good**. In fact, this is God's great commandment to us: love your enemies means transform a relationship of evil into a relationship of good.

"One of the greatest gifts you can give to yourself is to

expand your identity,

to realize that you are not limited by anything you have been," says Tony Robbins. Transformation is identity expansion, the shattering of past barriers, the transcending of limits, the dawn of a new era within our hearts.

The Transformation makes Christianity "this wordly." Rather than place our hopes in an afterlife, we learn to transform our fears **into flowerbeds** and our sorrows **into sugarplums**.

If transformation is the quintessence of the Christian faith, then we can develop a more palpable definition of what it means to say, "I trust." Trust is the recognition that these Gospel texts have the capacity to transform us. To say, "I trust in Jesus" is not to say, "The Gospel myths are historically accurate," or "Jesus supernaturally intervenes in the affairs of men." It is to say, rather, "I trust that there is some kind of spark, something magical in this wisdom tradition that can impact my life. Right here. Right now."

Now we know why we cultivate a "personal relationship" with the Cosmic Christ. It is not for salvation. Not for eternal life. Not to go to Heaven. Not to avoid Hell. Not to prove that our beliefs are superior. It is, quite simply, to be transformed. The only Hell is the self that we cannot transform.

The Transformation is the Great Christian l'chaim to life! The Transformation leads us to fulfillment here on earth, as close as we will ever come to Paradise. By living in the "eternal now" as Tillich calls it, we affirm the eternity of our beings. With the Transformation as the locus of Christian spirituality, there are no end times, no last judgment, no second coming: the Transformation is the

Great Christian Yes!

Our spiritual mentors are great transformers. We reckon our lives before and after them. The great theologians of our millennium—or indeed of any millennium—are the transformation theologians. Every soul can transform, start over, become a child again—this is the Good News of the Cosmic Christ.

MIDRASH:

NO NEED TO BELIEVE

In his marvelous book, *So You Think You're Not Religious: A Thinking Person's Guide To The Church*, James Adams tells the inspiring story of how he came to a deeper appreciation of the Christian faith. While attending a series of lectures at Oxford University, he discovered that in the early years of the Church, credo meant,

"I lend my heart to."

It did not mean, as we so often mistranslate it today, "I believe." The early Christians did not say, "I believe in Jesus"; instead they said, "I lend my heart to Jesus."

Today our dictionaries define creed as "a set of beliefs" or "a summary of the principles of the Christian faith." The original meaning of creed and credo have been entirely lost. The vast majority of English translations misleadingly insert the word "believe" where "trust" or "confidence" would be more accurate. They conform to doctrines and orthodoxies that emerged centuries after Jesus died. The Scholars Version beautifully restores these lost meanings. (See, for example, Mark 1:15, 4:40, 5:34, 9:24, 10:52 and 11:22.)

We can appreciate how critical the translation is and how easily it can drive away spiritual seekers of the new millennium, who simply cannot "believe" in the Bible in any conventional way. According to a recent Christian Retail Publishing report, a handful of conservative evangelical and fundamentalist publishers own 98% of the Bible market in North America. This means that the footnotes and commentary of almost every Bible you buy is filled with outdated assertions such as, "The Bible is the inspired Word of God, inerrant in the original manuscripts. It is the only means of knowing God's specific plan of salvation and His will for life." We desperately need Bibles that focus on love and forgiveness and good works, not exclusivist dogmas and doctrines; Bibles that inspire us to trust, not believe; Bibles that beautifully restore the lost spiritual meanings and lost spiritual worlds of the early Church.

http://www.noneedtobelieve.com **Mark 9: 14-24**

[14]When they rejoined the disciples, they saw a huge crowd surrounding them and scholars arguing with them. [15]And all of a sudden, when the whole crowd caught sight of him, they were alarmed and rushed up to meet him. [16]He asked them, "Why are you bothering to argue with them?" [17]And one person from the crowd answered him, "Teacher, I brought my son to you, because he has a mute spirit. [18]Whenever it takes him over, it knocks him down, and he foams at the mouth and grinds his teeth and stiffens up. I asked your disciples to drive it out, but they couldn't." [19]In response he says, "You distrustful lot, how long must I associate with you? How long must I put up with you? Bring him over to me!" [20]And they brought him over to him. And when the spirit noticed him, right away it threw him into convulsions, and he fell to the ground, and kept rolling around, foaming at the mouth. [21]And (Jesus) asked his father, "How long has he been like this?" He replied, "Ever since he was a child. [22]Frequently it has thrown him into fire and into water to destroy him. So if you can do anything, take pity on us and help us!" [23]Jesus said to him, "What do you mean, 'If you can'?

ALL THINGS ARE **POSSIBLE** FOR THE ONE WHO **TRUSTS**."

[24]Right away the father of the child cried out and said, "I do trust! Help my lack of

TRUST!"

Mark 9: 25-37 🌐 http://www.warpspeed.smile

²⁵When Jesus saw that the crowd was about to mob them, he rebuked the unclean spirit, and commands it, "Deaf and mute spirit, I command you, get out of him and don't ever go back inside him!" ²⁶And after he shrieked and went into a series of convulsions, it came out. And he took on the appearance of a corpse, so that the rumor went around that he had died. ²⁷But Jesus took hold of his hand and raised him, and there he stood.

²⁸And when he had gone home, his disciples started questioning him privately: "Why couldn't we drive it out?" ²⁹He said to them, "The only thing that can drive this kind out is prayer."

³⁰They left there and started going through Galilee, and he did not want anyone to know. ³¹Remember, he was instructing his disciples and telling them: "The son of Adam is being turned over to his enemies, and they will end up killing him. And three days after he is killed he will rise!" ³²But they never understood this remark, and always dreaded to ask him (about it). ³³And they came to Capernaum. When he got home, he started questioning them, "What were you arguing about on the road?" ³⁴They fell completely silent, because on the road they had been bickering about who was greatest. ³⁵He sat down and called the twelve and says to them, "If any of you wants to be 'number one,' you have to be last of all and servant of all!" ³⁶And he took a child and had her stand in front of them, and he put his arm around her, and he said to them,

³⁷"WHOEVER ACCEPTS A CHILD,

like this in my name is accepting me. And whoever accepts me is not so much accepting me as the one who sent me."

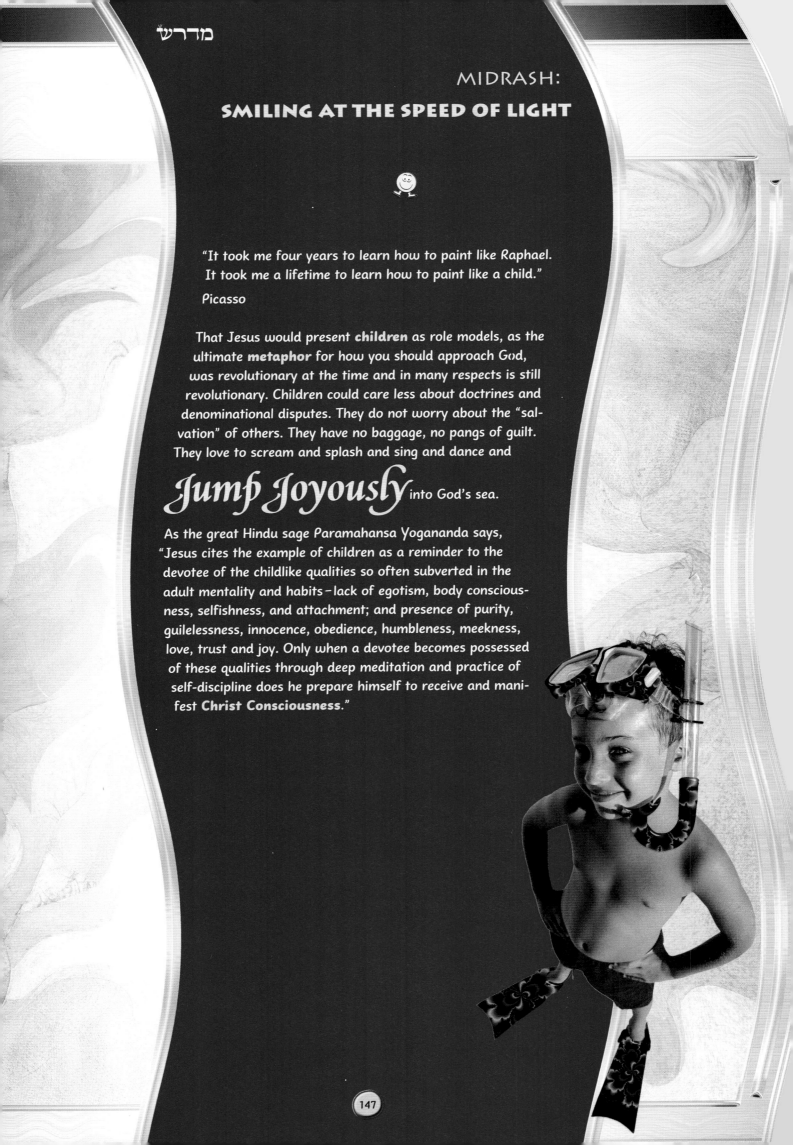

MIDRASH:

SMILING AT THE SPEED OF LIGHT

"It took me four years to learn how to paint like Raphael. It took me a lifetime to learn how to paint like a child."

Picasso

That Jesus would present **children** as role models, as the ultimate **metaphor** for how you should approach God, was revolutionary at the time and in many respects is still revolutionary. Children could care less about doctrines and denominational disputes. They do not worry about the "salvation" of others. They have no baggage, no pangs of guilt. They love to scream and splash and sing and dance and

Jump Joyously into God's sea.

As the great Hindu sage Paramahansa Yogananda says, "Jesus cites the example of children as a reminder to the devotee of the childlike qualities so often subverted in the adult mentality and habits — lack of egotism, body consciousness, selfishness, and attachment; and presence of purity, guilelessness, innocence, obedience, humbleness, meekness, love, trust and joy. Only when a devotee becomes possessed of these qualities through deep meditation and practice of self-discipline does he prepare himself to receive and manifest **Christ Consciousness**."

MIDRASH:
WHEN YOU STUMBLE, SMILE

The King James Version famously translates Mark 9:47 as, "If thine eye offend thee, pluck it out." There is no English equivalent for the Greek word σκανδαλίζης. It means to offend or cause to stumble, and is the origin of the word "scandalize."

A militant minority of fundamentalists claim to read the Bible literally yet **refuse** to read Mark 9:47 literally. They are scandalized by whoever and whatever offends them. Much sooner do they pursue the straight and narrow path, seeking to cut off and pluck out and rip out from our culture people with different views, than to love them for who they are, as Jesus repeatedly taught.

A metaphorical reading of this passage yields a far more healthy kind of spiritual fruit: when you stumble, Jesus says,

Smile
and work on yourself.

"Pluck out your eye" means pluck out the offense within. If what you see bothers you, put on a new pair of spiritual glasses and **focus on correcting your own vision**. Do not proselytize or pretend that your vision is superior. Treat others with love and respect. Transform yourself and focus on helping the "little trusting souls" of the world, as Jesus advises.

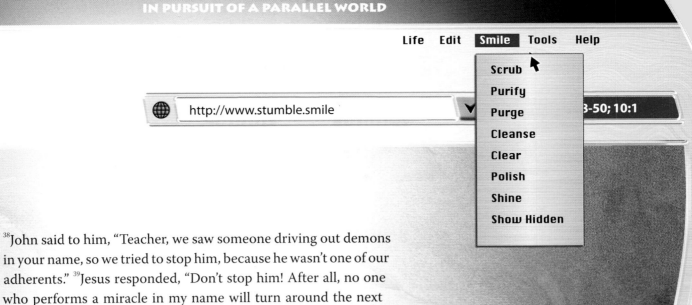

Life   Edit   **Smile**   Tools   Help

Scrub
Purify
Purge
Cleanse
Clear
Polish
Shine
Show Hidden

http://www.stumble.smile

3-50; 10:1

[38]John said to him, "Teacher, we saw someone driving out demons in your name, so we tried to stop him, because he wasn't one of our adherents." [39]Jesus responded, "Don't stop him! After all, no one who performs a miracle in my name will turn around the next moment and curse me. [40]In fact, whoever is not against us is on our side. [41]By the same token, whoever gives you a cup of water to drink because you carry the name of the Anointed, I swear to you, such a person certainly won't go un rewarded! [42]"And any of you who misleads one of these **LITTLE TRUSTING SOULS** would be better off if you had a millstone hung around your neck and were thrown into the sea! [43]"And if your hand gets you into trouble,

CUT IT OFF!

It's better for you to enter life maimed than to wind up in Gehenna, in the unquenchable fire, with both hands! [45]"And if your foot gets you into trouble,

CUT IT OFF!

It's better for you to enter life lame than to be thrown into Gehenna with both feet! [47]"And if your eye gets you into trouble,

RIP IT OUT!

It's better for you to enter God's domain one-eyed than to be thrown into Gehenna with both eyes, [48]where the worm never dies and the fire never goes out! [49]"As you know, everyone there is salted by fire. [50]"Salt is good (and salty) — if salt becomes bland, with what will you renew it? "Maintain 'salt' among yourselves and be at peace with one another." [10:1]And from there he gets up and goes to the territory of Judea and across the Jordan, and once again crowds gather around him.

As usual, he started teaching them. [2]And Pharisees approach him and, to test him, they ask whether a husband is permitted to divorce his wife. [3]In response he puts a question to them: "What did Moses command you?" [4]They replied, "Moses allowed one to prepare a writ of abandonment and thus to divorce the other party." [5]Jesus said to them, "He gave you this injunction because you are obstinate. [6]However, in the beginning, at the creation, 'God made them male and female.' [7]'For this reason, a man will leave his father and mother and be united with his wife, [8]and the two will become one person,' so they are no longer two individuals but 'one person.' [9]Therefore those God has coupled together, no one else should separate." [10]And once again, as usual, when they got home, the disciples questioned him about this. [11]And he says to them, "Whoever divorces his wife and marries another commits adultery against her; [12]and if she divorces her husband and marries another, she commits adultery." [13]And they would bring children to him so he could lay hands on them, but the disciples scolded them. [14]Then Jesus grew indignant when he saw this and said to them: "Let the children come up to me, don't try to stop them. After all, God's domain belongs to people like that. [15]I swear to you, whoever doesn't accept God's imperial rule the way a child would, certainly won't ever set foot in (his domain)!" [16]And he would put his arms around them and bless them, and lay his hands on them. [17]As he was traveling along the road, someone ran up, knelt before him, and started questioning him: "Good teacher, what do I have to do to inherit eternal life?" [18]Jesus said to him,

"WHY DO YOU CALL ME GOOD? NO ONE IS GOOD EXCEPT FOR GOD ALONE.

MIDRASH:
THE HUMBLE JESUS

Here Rabbi Jesus shows

remarkable Humility,

not even allowing his disciples and admirers to call him "good." Yet 2,000 years later, a militant minority is proclaiming him as not only good, not only as inspired by God, but as "the perfect son of God." Imagine if Mark 10:18 read, "Perfect Son of God, what shall I do to inherit eternal life?" How **disappointed** the historical Jesus would have been! The young man simply said, "Good teacher." And Jesus had trouble with even this.

The Gospel of **Matthew**, which was written a generation after Mark, **twisted Mark's wording** from "Why do you call me good?" to "Why do you ask me about the good?" (Matthew 19:17). It is a profound **shift in meaning**, yet one easily missed by all but the most careful readers. Matthew simply would not allow Jesus to express his own humility; that would mean—God forbid—that Jesus was just a man, just one of the sons of Adam, just like you and me.

"Wherever we emphasize the divinity of Jesus at the expense of his humanity, we lose track of the utterly remarkable human being that he was," writes Marcus Borg. "To deprive him of his humanity is to deprive him of his greatness." Of the 27 books canonized as the New Testament, Mark, above all, glorifies the flawed yet great humanity of Jesus.

The Prophet Muhammad said, "I am only a man like you" (Koran 18:110). **Humility** is a characteristic of all the great sages and founders of religions—including Jesus.

> **DOCTRINE ALERT!**
>
> In the Gospel of Mark (10:18), Jesus makes clear that we should not call him the "divine Son of God."

Mark 10: 19-31 http://www.exchange.energy

[19]You know the commandments: 'You must not murder, you are not to commit adultery, you are not to steal, you are not to give false testimony, you are not to defraud, and you are to honor your father and mother.'" [20]He said to him, "Teacher, I have observed all these things since I was a child!" [21]Jesus loved him at first sight and said to him, "You are missing one thing: make your move, sell whatever you have, and give (the proceeds) to the poor, and you will have treasure in heaven. And then come, follow me!" [22]But stunned by this advice, he went away dejected, since he possessed a fortune. [23]After looking around, Jesus says to his disciples, "How difficult it is for those who have money to enter God's domain!" [24]The disciples were

AMAZED

at his words. In response Jesus repeats what he had said, "Children, how difficult it is to enter God's domain! [25]It's easier for a camel to squeeze through a needle's eye than for a wealthy person to get into God's domain!" [26]And they were very

PERPLEXED,

wondering to themselves, "Well then, who can be saved?" [27]Jesus looks them in the eye and says, "For mortals it's impossible, but not for God; after all, everything's possible for God." [28]Peter started lecturing him: "Look at us, we left everything to follow you!" [29]Jesus said, "I swear to you, there is no one who has left home, or brothers, or sisters, or mother, or father, or children, or farms on my account and on account of the good news, [30]who won't receive a hundred times as much now, in the present time, homes, and brothers, and sisters, and mothers, and children, and farms — including persecutions — and in the age to come, eternal life. [31]"Many of the first will be last, and of the last many will be first."

8:00 PM

MIDRASH:
THE AMAZING BLESSING

Long before the birth of Jesus, in the sunrise days of Jacob and Solomon, Jews believed that wealth was a sign of God's favor. Rabbi Jesus shocked his disciples by saying no: your bank account is no reflection of your spiritual account. You can be wealthy on the outside but impoverished inside. This was shocking because it challenged a thousand years of Biblical wisdom. Jesus' revolutionary perspective on **spiritual wealth** is often misunderstood as a call to live in poverty. It is a call, rather, to **detach** from your possessions and to recognize a loving heart as the greatest kind of wealth.

As the Hindu sage Yogananda explains, "It is not the possessions of a rich man that destroy his God-consciousness, but his mental enslavement of being possessed by his possessions. There are persons who have been

blessed with prosperity,

who serve as examples of true seekers of God-consciousness, and who, with Christ-like compassion help to relieve the miseries of others. They utilize their good fortune in the right way."

MIDRASH:

SAINTS IN SHEEPS' CLOTHING

154

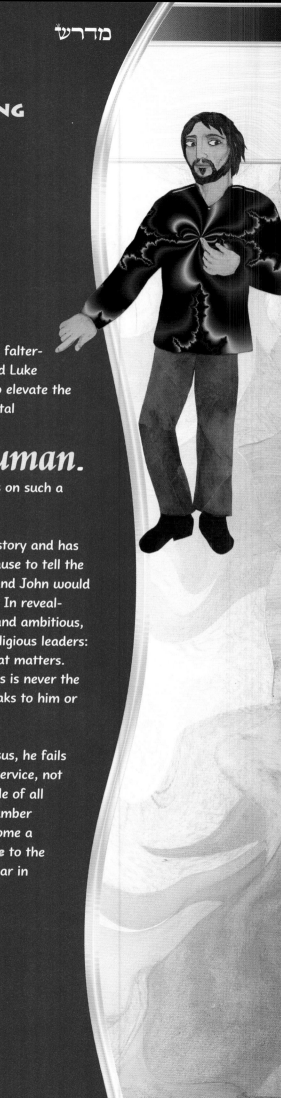

Throughout his Gospel, Mark shows the disciples faltering, doubting, selfish and conniving. Mathew and Luke whitewashed these critical moments, seeking to elevate the disciples to saintly status. Only Mark, with brutal honesty, gives us such

permission to be human.

Mark never put the disciples or even Jesus on such a pedestal, as did the later church.

Matthew (20:20) **twists the facts** of this story and has their mother Salome make the request, because to tell the truth about the selfish infighting of James and John would supposedly demean their status as Apostles. In revealing that even John and James were selfish and ambitious, Mark issues a **poignant reminder** to our religious leaders: it is not who you know, but who you are, that matters. The person who is most favored in God's eyes is never the one who egotistically proclaims that God speaks to him or through him, as so many televangelists do.

Whenever someone asserts the greatness of Jesus, he fails to follow his teachings. Greatness comes from service, not assertion. The true Christian humbly serves people of all faiths and does not vainly assert that Jesus is "number one." The one true way of the **Christian** is to become a **slave** to the Buddhist, a **slave** to the Hindu, a **slave** to the Muslim, and a **slave** to the Jew, as Jesus makes clear in verses 43 and 44.

http://www.spirituality.paradox

Mark 10: 32-45

[32]On the road going up to Jerusalem, Jesus was leading the way, they were apprehensive, and others who were following were frightened. Once again he took the twelve aside and started telling them what was going to happen to him: [33]"Listen, we're going up to Jerusalem, and the son of Adam will be turned over to the ranking priests and the scholars, and they will sentence him to death, and turn him over to foreigners, [34]and they will make fun of him, and spit on him, and flog him, and put (him) to death. Yet after three days he will rise!" [35]Then James and John, the sons of Zebedee, come up to him, and say to him, "Teacher, we want you to do for us whatever we ask!" [36]He said to them, "What do you want me to do for you?" [37]They reply to him, **"IN YOUR GLORY, LET ONE OF US SIT AT YOUR RIGHT HAND, AND THE OTHER AT YOUR LEFT."** [38]Jesus said to them, "You have no idea what you're asking for. Can you drink the cup that I'm drinking, or undergo the baptism I'm undergoing?" [39]They said to him, "We can!" Jesus said to them, "The cup I'm drinking you'll be drinking, and the baptism I'm undergoing you'll be undergoing, [40]but as for sitting at my right or my left, that's not mine to grant, but belongs to those for whom it has been reserved." [41]When they learned of it, the ten got **ANNOYED** with James and John. [42]So, calling them aside, Jesus says to them: "You know how those who supposedly rule over foreigners lord it over them, and how their strong men tyrannize them. [43]It's not going to be like that with you! With you, **WHOEVER WANTS TO BECOME GREAT MUST BE YOUR SERVANT,** [44]and whoever among you wants to be 'number one' must be

EVERYBODY'S
SLAVE.

[45]After all, the son of Adam didn't come to be served, but to serve, even to give his life as a ransom for many."

[46]Then they come to Jericho. As he was leaving Jericho with his disciples and a sizable crowd, Bartimaeus, a blind beggar, the son of Timaeus, was sitting alongside the road. [47]When he learned that it was Jesus the Nazarene, he began to shout: "You son of David, Jesus, have mercy on me!" [48]And many kept yelling at him to shut up, but he shouted all the louder, "You son of David, have mercy on me!" [49]Jesus paused and said, "Tell him to come over here!" They called to the blind man, "Be brave, get up, he's calling you!" [50]So he threw off his cloak, and jumped to his feet, and went over to Jesus. [51]In response Jesus said, "What do you want me to do for you?" The blind man said to him, "Rabbi, **I WANT TO SEE AGAIN!**" [52]And Jesus said to him, "Be on your way,

YOUR TRUST,
HAS **CURED** YOU."

And right away he regained his sight, and he started following him on the road.

MIDRASH:
CREATING A MIRACLE WITHIN

We third millennium readers are blind whenever we read the Bible literally—blind because we cannot believe. It is only when we **stop trying** to read it historically or factually, when we **stop projecting** a postmodern, scientific perspective onto a first century spiritual text, that

the veil is lifted

and we can see the deeper truths of Scripture.

Where the blind man says, in Mark 10:51, "I want to see again!" it now means: "I want to **discover** the treasures of our Lost Spiritual World. I want to **experience** the Godliness to which our ancestors aspired, but I want to experience it authentically and credibly, as a third millennium seeker and devotee of science. It also means that I want to see the good in every situation, to inspire and uplift others, and to flood my soul with love and joy."

Read this passage carefully. Notice that Jesus never says, "I have cured you." He simply says, "**Your trust** has cured you." This was his greatest gift—not performing supernatural miracles but inspiring people to create a miracle within. As Emerson said, "Jesus speaks always from within, and in a degree that transcends all others. In that is the miracle."

MIDRASH:

TO THE STARS THROUGH THE MUD

In the days of Jesus, there was no consensus among the
Jews as to whether or when a Messiah would ever come.
Echoing the prophesies of Daniel (7:13) and Zachariah (9:9),
the Talmud claimed, "If the people are worthy, he will come
through the clouds of Heaven; if they are unworthy, he
will come like a poor man riding on a donkey." The Gospel
writers changed "donkey" to "colt" because they thought
it demeaning that the Messiah would arrive on a donkey,
whereas a colt was emblematic of Roman royalty. Yet the
deep spiritual lesson is precisely that he would arrive on a
donkey. Jesus was anointed to deliver what was—and still is
—a desperately needed message of love and forgiveness
to the world. Even still, this "son of Adam" was not destined
to fly first class. An ass, not a Lear jet, it would be.

How many times have you had to ride a donkey (metaphorically speaking), endure hardship when you knew in your heart
that you deserved so much better? In Hebrew, Zachariah
calls the man on a donkey a צדיק (tzadik), which most
translations oversimplify as "a righteous man." But a צדיק is
so much more: he or she rides the waves of life with perfect
equanimity, putting service before selfishness and kindness
before competition.

Rabbi Jesus was a צדיק, the highest of the high, yet here
he was riding an ass in what was supposed to be his trium-
phant moment. The mark of greatness is to make the most
of what you have. And not to laugh at those who pursue
their *Angelic visions,*
even if they have to do so on a donkey.

There is an old Latin saying: per aspera ad astra, to the stars
through the mud. That's how Jesus got there—and how many
of us will get there, too.

http://www.unorthodox.triumph

Mark 11: 1-11

[1]When they get close to Jerusalem, near Bethphage and Bethany at the Mount of Olives, he sends off two of his disciples [2]with these instructions: "Go into the village across the way, and right after you enter it, you'll find a colt tied up, one that has never been ridden. Untie it and bring it here. [3]If anyone questions you, 'Why are you doing this?' tell them, 'Its master has need of it and he will send it back here right away.'" [4]They set out and found a colt tied up at the door out on the street, and they untie it. [5]Some of the people standing around started saying to them, "What do you think you're doing, untying that colt?" [6]But they said just what Jesus had told them to say, so they left them alone. [7]So they bring the colt to Jesus, and they throw their cloaks over it; then he got on it. [8]And many people spread their cloaks on the road, while others cut leafy branches from the fields. [9]Those leading the way and those following kept shouting, "Hosanna!

BLESSED

is the one who comes in the name of the Lord!" [10]Blessed is the coming kingdom of our father David! "Hosanna" in the highest! [11]And he went into Jerusalem to the temple area and took stock of everything, but, since the hour was already late, he returned to Bethany with the twelve.

Mark 11: 12-14 http://www.radiation.spirit

12 On the next day, as they were leaving Bethany, he got hungry. 13 So
when he spotted a fig tree in the distance with some leaves on it,
he went up to it expecting to find something on it. But when he
got right up to it, he found nothing on it except some leaves. (You
see, it wasn't 'time' for figs.) 14 And he

REACTED

by saying: "May no one so much as taste your fruit again!"
And his disciples were listening.

MIDRASH:
AUTHENTICITY

This is one of the most revealing passages in all of Scripture, for Mark shows Jesus hungry and selfish and using his miraculous powers to extract vengeance on a fig tree whose fruits were out of season. This memorable little incident is out of character with the Jesus we know and love and is a testimony to the **honesty** of Mark. Jesus was a man who hungered physically and whose behavior was sometimes reprehensible. Just because Jesus was one of the "favored sons" of God does not mean he was beyond reproach.

One has to wonder why, if Jesus was such a miracle man, he could not get the fig tree to yield fruit out of season. Instead of using his supposedly supernatural powers to nourish himself, he inflicts vengeance on a harmless tree. He walks away hungry and the tree dies—a lose lose situation. Mark definitely wants us to know this story for a reason: **Jesus** may have been divinely inspired, but like Moses and David he was a

flawed human being
—just like the rest of us.*

Mark's willingness to share this story is one of the gems of the New Testament; it is why Christianity is difficult to transcend, even in the third millennium. The story challenges the exousia, the authority of Jesus; yet this challenge grants him an even **greater authority through its authenticity.** Authority comes not from doctrinal submission but from authenticity, even vulnerability. No matter how exalted someone's position in life, no matter how great their power or how many revere them, they are still capable—like Jesus —of egotistical, destructive behavior. We can open our Bibles, point to the story of the fig tree, and say to the authorities, "If even Jesus Christ was capable of poor judgment, then so are you."

*If the fundamentalists insist on a symbolic reading of this passage, e.g. the fig tree "symbolizes" a sinful Jerusalem, then they undermine the very literalism to which they cling.

Mark 11: 15-18 http://www.darkmatter.doctrine

[15]They come to Jerusalem. And he went into the temple and began chasing the vendors and shoppers out of the temple area, and he turned the bankers' tables upside down, along with the chairs of the pigeon merchants, [16]and he wouldn't even let anyone carry a container through the temple area. [17]Then he started teaching and would say to them: "Don't the scriptures say, 'My house is to be regarded as **A HOUSE OF PRAYER FOR ALL PEOPLES**? — but you have turned it into 'a hideout for

CROOKS'!"

[18]And the ranking priests and the scholars heard this and kept looking for a way to get rid of him. (The truth is that they stood in fear of him, and that the whole crowd was

ASTONISHED

at his teaching.)

The overturning of the tables in the Temple is a violent scene, captured brilliantly by Rembrandt on pages 164-165. It was so violent, in fact, that many scholars believe the real reason for Jesus' crucifixion was the riot he caused in the Temple, which Mark refers to again in verse 15:7. The doctrine of "vicarious atonement," e.g. the idea that Jesus died for our sins, emerged only much later in Church history. A recent cover story in America's leading evangelical magazine, Christianity Today (May 2006), questioned whether Christ really "died" for our "sins." The article had the tagline, "More and more evangelicals believe Christ's atoning death is merely a grotesque creation of the medieval imagination."

Behind Jesus' righteous indignation is a remarkably ecumenical Spirit. In quoting Isaiah 56:7, he did not say, "This is a house of prayer for the Jews," or, "This is a house of prayer for the Gentiles." He said, "This is a house of prayer

for all peoples."

Sadly, these desperately needed, pluralistic words of Jesus are being ignored by a highly visible, militant minority of fundamentalists who do not want America to be a house of prayer for all peoples. They are pressuring us to adopt certain beliefs and religious practices, just as a greedy minority in the Roman Catholic Church once pressured people to purchase indulgences. "Buy or be damned" and "Believe or be damned" (or more gently, "Buy your way to Heaven" or "Believe your way to Heaven") are the same phenomena, in a different guise. To adapt something Yogi Bera once said: it's déja vu, indulgences all over again.

In quoting Isaiah 56:7, Jesus was simply affirming the pluralism of his day. As the scholar Bart Ehrman explains in Lost Christianities, "The Roman Empire was populated with religions of all kinds: family religions, local religions, city religions, state religions... Worship never involved accepting or making doctrinally acceptable claims about a god. There were no creeds devised to proclaim the true nature of the gods and the interaction with the world."

The belief that America is a "Christian nation" or that Jesus Christ is the only path to salvation has become a new kind of political indulgence. As Jon Meacham explains in his brilliant book, American Gospel, "The Right's contention that we are a 'Christian nation' that has fallen from pure origins and can achieve redemption by some kind of return to Christian values is based on **wishful thinking**, not convincing historical argument."

Indeed, in an early treaty with the Muslim nation of Tripoli, ratified by the Senate in 1797 and signed by John Adams, the Founders wrote that "the government of the United States is not in any sense founded on the Christian Religion." For the Founding Fathers, writes Meacham, "Jesus of Nazareth was a

Great moral teacher

—even the greatest in all history—but he was not the Son of God; the Holy Trinity was seen as an invention of a corrupt church more interested in temporal power than in true religion."

Thomas Jefferson stated openly that he did not believe in original sin, the resurrection, miracles, the trinity or the supernatural. "Among the sayings and discourses imputed to (Jesus) by his biographers, I find many passages of fine imagination, correct morality, and of the most lovely benevolence; and others again of so much ignorance, so much absurdity, so much **untruth, charlatanism,** and imposture, as to pronounce it impossible that such contradictions should have proceeded from the same being," he said.

Jefferson created a beautiful version of the Gospels that cut the nonsensical verses (which he believed were added by later writers) and focused on the moral and ethical teachings of the Cosmic Christ. The Jefferson Bible was once given as an official gift to all incoming members of Congress. George Washington said, "We have abundant reason to rejoice that in the Land the light of truth and reason has triumphed over the power of bigotry and superstition." Yet at this critical time in world history, America risks becoming a **land of bigotry and superstition**—exactly what Washington and Jefferson and especially Jesus would have abhorred. A "den of bigots" is how many people from around the world are describing our nation today.

I recently saw a bumper sticker that said, "God is a Republican." None of our wisdom traditions—especially Christianity—teach or encourage this kind of bigotry and ignorance. The Kingdom of God is a **spiritual ideal**, a cry from the wilderness to transform our hearts, to reconcile with our neighbors. It is not an instrument of realpolitik.

We need not know the how of peace to understand the why of peace. We need only believe that in every crisis there is hope. We are the

voices that cry

in the wilderness. Now is the time for us to be the peace and show the love of which the old prophets could only dream.

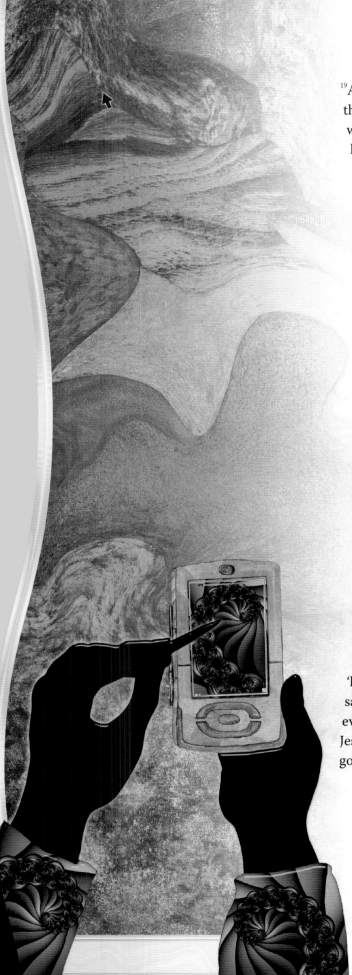

[19]And when it grew dark, they made their way out of the city. [20]As they were walking along early one morning, they saw the fig tree withered from the roots up. [21]And Peter remembered and says to him: "Rabbi, look, the fig tree you cursed has withered up!" [22]In response Jesus says to them: "Have trust in God. [23]I swear to you, those who say to this mountain, 'Up with you and into the sea!' and **DO NOT WAVER IN THEIR CONVICTION,** but **TRUST THAT WHAT THEY SAY WILL HAPPEN,** that's the way it will be. [24]This is why I keep telling you,

TRUST

that you will receive everything you pray and ask for, and that's the way it will turn out. [25]And when you stand up to pray, if you are holding anything against anyone,

FORGIVE

them, so your Father in heaven may FORGIVE your misdeeds." [27]Once again they come to Jerusalem. As he walks around in the temple area, the ranking priests and scholars and elders come up to him [28]and start questioning him: "By what right are you doing these things?" or, "Who gave you the authority to do these things?" [29]But Jesus said to them: "I have one question for you. If you answer me, then I will tell you by what authority I do these things. [30]Tell me, was the baptism of John heaven-sent or was it of human origin? Answer me that." [31]And they conferred among themselves, saying, "If we say 'heaven-sent,' he'll say, 'Then why didn't you trust him?' [32]But if we say 'Of human origin ... !'" They were afraid of the crowd. (You see, everybody considered John a genuine prophet.) [33]So they answered Jesus by saying, "We can't tell." And Jesus says to them: "I'm not going to tell you by what authority I do these things either!"

MIDRASH:
MOUNTAIN MOVERS

Jesus deserves far more credit for his spiritual explorations of existing Jewish sayings than for originating the sayings commonly – and mistakenly – attributed to him. The most famous saying often mistakenly attributed to Jesus is, "Love thy neighbor as thyself," which predates Jesus by at least 1,500 years and is preserved in the Torah (Leviticus 19:18).

"If you have faith, you can move mountains" was likewise a common rabbinic saying and did not originate with Jesus. In fact, many rabbis were called "mountain movers" for their ability to remove the mental and *Spiritual Mountains* of their students.

Think of the angels, the mountain movers who come into your life. They teach you to bury your troubles in a mountain of gratitude. They teach you to trust and forgive. They even teach you to love those who stand as a mountain against you. Loving your enemies is the tallest mountain, the hardest to climb; but if you can tap into the power of love, the world is yours, and the mountains are mere stepping stones.

MIDRASH:

THE JOYS OF REJECTION

When the prophet Samuel announced that one of Jesse's sons was to be anointed king, no one even considered David, a "mere" shepherd. David was rejected by his own family; later, in Psalm 118:22, he wrote, "A stone that the builders rejected has ended up as the keystone." Jesus cites this inspiring verse to remind you that whenever you feel rejected, drowning in the waves, there is still a divine destiny waiting for you.

It seems like a law of human nature that the world rejects its keystones. But rejection by the Establishment is good. Rejection says: "Either walk away or deepen your resolve. If you walk away, it was never meant to be; but if you deepen your resolve, then the rejection was sent to strengthen you. The rejection builds your **commitment muscles**. Now is the time to

MAKE
YOURSELF
UNSTOPPABLE –
stronger than you were before."

I once had a pile of over 800 rejection letters from agents and publishers who insisted that there will never be a **Renaissance of beautifully designed books** and that reading will always be a rectangular, black and white experience! How they laughed at the wavy edges! How they insisted that the book you now hold in your hands would be "impossible to print or publish"! I now see their rejections as the joyous seeds that led me to the Lost Spiritual World series. How grateful I am for their rejections!

Joan Chittister writes of that divine moment when we move "beyond fear of loss and fear of others to a sense of spiritual invincibility, to the awareness that nothing and no one can deter us from what we are meant to do."

http://www.spiritual.cortex ▼ **Mark 12: 1-11**

¹And he began to speak to them in parables: Someone planted a vineyard, put a hedge around it, dug a winepress, built a tower, leased it out to some farmers, and went abroad. ²In due time he sent a slave to the farmers to collect his share of the vineyard's crop from them. ³But they grabbed him, beat him, and sent him away empty-handed. ⁴So once again he sent another slave to them, but they attacked him and abused him. ⁵Then he sent another, and this one they killed; many others followed, some of whom they beat, others of whom they killed. ⁶He still had one more, a son who was the apple of his eye. This one he finally sent to them, with the thought, "They will show this son of mine some respect." ⁷But those farmers said to one another, "This fellow's the heir! Come on, let's kill him and the inheritance will be ours!" ⁸So they grabbed him, and killed him, and threw him outside the vineyard. ⁹What will the owner of the vineyard do? He will come in person, and do away with those farmers, and give the vineyard to someone else. ¹⁰Haven't you read this scripture, A stone that the builders

has ended up as the keystone. ¹¹It was the Lord's doing and is something you admire?

REJECTED

[12](His opponents) kept looking for some opportunity to seize him, but they were still afraid of the crowd, since they realized that he had aimed the parable at them. So they left him there and went on their way. [13]And they send some of the Pharisees and the Herodians to him to trap him with a riddle. [14]They come and say to him, "Teacher, we know that you are honest and impartial, because you pay no attention to appearances, but instead you teach God's way forthrightly. Is it permissible to pay the poll tax to the Roman emperor or not? Should we pay or should we not pay?" [15]But he saw through their trap, and said to them, "Why do you provoke me like this? Let me have a look at a coin." [16]They handed him a silver coin, and he says to them, "Whose picture is this? Whose name is on it?" They replied, "The emperor's." [17]Jesus said to them:

"PAY THE EMPEROR **WHAT BELONGS** TO THE EMPEROR, AND GOD **WHAT BELONGS** TO GOD!"

And they were **DUMBFOUNDED** at him.

MIDRASH:
SPIRITUAL BLACK HOLES

For the first 11 chapters, we just assumed the exousia, the authority of Science—did we not? Our critique of literalism and our creation of new metaphors have been inspired by psychology, neuroscience, quantum physics and linguistics. We are grateful for Science, but what exactly is its authority in our lives? Dare we even question it? Is Science the **soul's new Caesar?** Will we soon capitalize Science, as we now capitalize God?

The third millennium seeker asks the Cosmic Christ, "What belongs to Science and what to God?" And the answer is, "Render unto Science what belongs to Science and unto God what belongs to God." The question, then, is what belongs to Science and what to God?

When it comes to Science, I can only echo Montaigne—Que sais-je? Who am I? What do I know? I cannot speak with any exousia, any authority about Science. But this is the whole point, is it not? **Few of us can speak about Science** with exousia. Yet we must live, work, think and decide in a scientific age. Despite the publicity surrounding backward school districts that attempt to teach creationism or intelligent design in the classroom, the truth is this: Science is winning—and winning big—in shaping our worldview, including our spiritual view. Allowing Science to run rampant inside our souls is like giving one branch of government all the power.

The first passage of the famous Jewish treatise, Ethics of Our Fathers, tells us to "make a fence (mechitzah) around the Torah." Likewise, we need to make a mechitzah, a

fence around the Soul.

The First Amendment of spirituality is the Soul's right to privacy. This includes privacy from analysis, from reduction, from explanation—from Science.

"Religion is the human longing for something beyond the world, the discovery of another sphere where only the soul can abide," said Bultmann. This is exactly what we need: **a sphere where only the soul**—and not Science or government or religious doctrine—can abide. The last preserve of freedom is the

undigitized self,

the self as informationless, as neither a one nor a zero, neither a yes nor a know; the self as **ineffable, ambiguous, undefined**—mysterious. This is the Christ Zone, the Anointed Zone, where no instrument, no piercing ray of Science, no crucifix of materialism, no blood of reductionism dare enter. Otherwise Christ will become a new archetype—the crucifixion of the private self, the unknowable self, the self that is lost in explanation.

Analysis is a **spiritual black hole**, if it be carried too far. Explanation is a **spiritual black hole**, if it be carried too far. The soul needs a room of her own—a "sweet spot" as the evangelical Christian Max Lucado calls it—a place where no scientific instrument ever dare probe. The third Zen patriarch said, "The more you talk and think about it, the further away you wander from the truth. **Stop talking** and thinking, and there is nothing you will not be able to know." What Science does—and rightly so, for this is its Imperial Kingdom—is talk, analyze, explain, elaborate and invent. What religion does—at its best—is teach you to be still, receptive to the deeper mysteries. "True religion lies within oneself, in the cave of stillness, in the cave of calm intuitive wisdom, in the cave of the spiritual eye," says Paramahansa Yogananda.

A myth "allows us to make a journey we could otherwise not make, past all categories of definition," said Joseph Campbell. We would hardly benefit from Science creating a universe where everything is defined, explained, reduced and understood. To live as reductionists or atheists, to not have myths in our lives is to turn our backs on the historical continuum of which we are unavoidably a part. As frustrated as we may be at times with organized religions, we should be all the more grateful for their survival. They provide a desperately needed **release** from our reductionist, materialist mindset. They make us aware of the inadequacy of our scientific thinking and of the primacy—in the spiritual realm, at least—of mythical thinking. When we try to use reason to explain myth or Science to refute it, we miss the point. Mythical thinking respects the unknowable,

unexplainable realm

of spirit, where God dwells. Lao Tzu captured this beautifully in the Tao Te Ching (14):

"Looked at, but cannot be seen—
that is called the **invisible** (yi)
Listened to, but cannot be heard—
That is called the **inaudible** (his)
Grasped at, but cannot be touched—
That is called the **intangible** (wei).

Echoing Lao Tzu, the Apostle Paul described our faith as "the substance of things hoped for, the evidence of things not seen." The Bhagavad Gita likewise sings of "that infinite happiness that is realized by the purified heart, but is **beyond the grasp** of the senses." Gandhi, by no means a religious man, often spoke of "an indefinable mysterious Power that pervades everything. I feel it, though I do not see it." In every aspect of human endeavor, whether in East or West, whether in politics, religion, spirituality or Science, we confront this indefinable Mysterious Power.

The fall of third millennium man is his inability to recover the symbolic space of pre-Enlightenment man. **Paradise Lost** is **Spirituality Lost**. Scientific enlightenment is glorious, provided we do not lose our capacity to take deep spiritual dives. The purpose of our wisdom traditions is to captivate us, mesmerize us in the Homeric sense and transform us in the Markan sense. Even a nonbeliever and staunch empiricist such as Carl Jung could describe God as "a power and a meaning not yet understood." Jung warned atheists of a "serious undervaluation of the human soul."

God is "as powerful and as awe-inspiring as ever," says Jung. "The idea of God represents an important, even overwhelming psychic intensity." This *psychic intensity* never disappears; it only transforms. The quantum energy of the God of the first and second millenniums is still here, still present; we need only tap into it. We all have wired within ourselves "an archetypal image of the Deity," says Jung. We should never allow Science to sabotage our archetypes. The Cosmic Christ is still an **extraordinary archetype**: killing him would be like severing the aorta from the heart of man and womankind. Better that we stand on the shoulders of Science and infuse our religions with new rituals and new traditions that resonate in the third millennium.

To say that our great myths are not real is absurd. These myths bring **love** and **joy** and **hope** into the present and burnish a presence within us. They give birth to what the poets call the soul and what the scientists cannot reduce to material form. If Science cannot yet describe the transcendent spiritual forces of the Universe, how then can we best describe them, other than through metaphor and myth?

Just as the unconscious dreams, the conscious mytholo-
gizes. A myth is a conscious dream, a crystallization of the
mysterium tremendum. There is nothing wrong with saying,
in this year of the Cosmic Christ, 2006, that concerning
spiritual matters, **mythical thinking** is still superior to scientific thinking. It may be that in a few decades, or a few
centuries, scientific thinking will surpass mythical thinking,
but certainly not in this generation. A sterile environment
is good for Science but a black hole for the heart. On the
operating table, we may prefer Science; but in the fleshy
tables of our hearts, we still prefer myth.

In persuading the atheist C.S. Lewis to become a Christian,
J.R.R. Tolkien said, "I believe that **legends and myths** are
largely made of truth, and indeed present aspects of it that
can only be perceived in this mode. Long ago certain truths
and modes of this kind were discovered and must always
appear." Tolkien nicely captured a timeless truth about the
Bible: it preserves a critically important

mode of perception,

a mode lost
when the Church Fathers sought to embalm Jesus in doctrine and the Enlightenment fathers sought to marginalize
Jesus as little more than a spiritual black hole. If history
since the Enlightenment has taught us anything, it is that
we desperately need to recover this mode, for in it we
discover our deepest humanity. The Bible—the good parts,
at least—demand that we transform ourselves from selfish
Darwinian beasts into beacons of **love** and **hope**.

No less a scientist than J. Robert Oppenheimer said that scientists "live always at the **edge of mystery**." What makes us human is not only our capacity to further Science but to transform its mysteries into a spirituality we can live by. The unconscious, the emotional, the subjective, the inexact, the illogical, the symbolic, the contradictory, the ambiguous: these are all "characteristic of the human being at his highest levels of development as well as his lowest, and that they can be valued, used, loved, built upon, rather than just being swept under the rug," wrote Abraham Maslow.

I once thought I was an expert in my own body, a sibyl of feminine flesh, but now Science challenges even this belief —and has a point, does it not? I do not understand the inner workings of the trillions of neurons, synopses, membranes and cells that throb through me. I am humbled by the wonder of my own body and awed by the inability of our greatest minds to answer the simplest question: where did this flesh come from?

Myths become true the moment we feel them in the flesh. We can never fully explain our myths. We can only **live** them, **experience** them as God consciousness. To be a fully realized human being is to inhabit a myth, to allow our traditions to transform our hearts and to discipline our minds.

The Buddha said, "More than all your enemies, an untrained mind does greater harm. More than all your family, a well trained mind does greater good." If we live purely secular lives, and do not immerse ourselves in the great wisdom traditions, we often get sucked into the

spiritual black holes
of anger, hatred, narcissism, envy, selfishness and depression. All too often, Science leaves us stranded at the gates of our inner Heaven, materially prosperous yet spiritually impoverished, if not bankrupt.

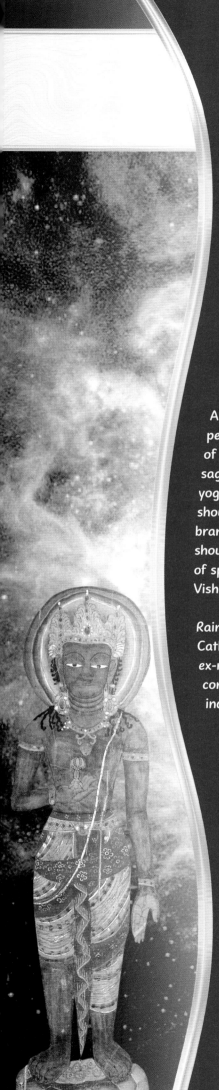

Recent findings in psychology confirm that without some higher level spiritual practice or discipline, "we are only half grown and half-awake," says Roger Walsh, a doctor and author of **Essential Spirituality**. "Spiritual practices can reduce stress, blood pressure and cholesterol levels. They may help alleviate insomnia, muscle spasms, and diseases ranging from migraine to chronic pain. They may even reduce the effects of aging and lengthen the life span."

A thousand years ago, the Sufi mystics understood this perfectly well. Their writings are **rapturous explorations** of the 'ilm al-qulub, the "Science of the Hearts." Hindu sages such as Yogananda likewise refer to the practice of yoga, meditation and mantras as a "Science." Perhaps we should think of our wisdom traditions not as religions but as branches of **Spiritual Science**. Just as Newton stood on the shoulders of the giants of Science, we stand on the shoulders of spiritual giants—Moses, Buddha, Muhammad, Lao-Tzu, Vishnu and Jesus.

Raimon Panikkar insightfully notes that there are "ex-Catholics, ex-Marxists, ex-Buddhists... but I know of no ex-mystics." Once you feel that special something, once you connect to this Energy Source in some magnificent and indescribable way,

you will

embrace the energy

for the rest of your life.

In the wake of all we may never know, humility is the one constant, the one bit of wisdom that protects us from the black holes of despair. "Do you know all the answers?" God asks Job. "Have you ever commanded the day to dawn?" Job answered, "I talked about things I did not understand, about marvels too great for me to know." Soon Science will send a man to Mars, but never will Science command the day to dawn. Science is marvelous, but there will always be marvels too great for us to know.

Mark 12: 18-27   http://www.enigma.url

[18]And some Sadducees — those who maintain

THERE IS NO RESURRECTION

— come up to him and they start questioning him. [19]"Teacher," they said, "Moses wrote for our benefit, 'If someone's brother dies and leaves his widow childless, his brother is obligated to take the widow as his wife and produce offspring for his brother.' [20]There were seven brothers; now the first took a wife but left no children when he died. [21]So the second married her but died without leaving offspring, and the third likewise. [22]In fact, all seven (married her but) left no offspring. Finally, the wife died too. [23]In the resurrection, after they rise, whose wife will she be?" (Remember, all seven had her as wife.) [24]Jesus said to them: "You've missed the point again, haven't you, all because you underestimate both the scriptures and the power of God. [25]After all, when men and women rise from the dead, they do not marry, but resemble heaven's messengers. [26]As for whether or not the dead are raised, haven't you read in the book of Moses in the passage about the bush, how God spoke to him: 'I am the God of Abraham and the God of Isaac and the God of Jacob'? [27]This is not the God of the dead, only of the living — you're constantly missing the point!"

מדרש

MIDRASH:

THE RESURRECTION AS POETRY

This is the only instance in which the Jews known as the Sadducees are mentioned in Mark. Like many of the earliest Christians—and most Jews and enlightened spiritual seekers of today—the Sadducees **did not believe** in bodily resurrection. As the great philosopher Karl Jaspers writes, "The Resurrection was just as implausible to the contemporaries of Jesus as it is to modern man." We are not alone in our skepticism and disbelief.

One of the joys of being alive today is that we can be inspired by Christianity without believing in the bodily resurrection of Jesus. A new generation of scholars and writers is rediscovering the **spiritual side** of ancient and medieval Christianity. Five hundred years ago, a devout Catholic woman expressed her love for Christ in some of the most

beautiful poetry

on the resurrection
ever written:

> Christ has no body now on earth but yours,
> No hands but yours, no feet but yours,
> Yours are the eyes through which his compassion
>   gazes upon the world;
> Yours are the feet with which he does good;
> Yours are the hands with which he blesses men and
>   women now.

Saint Teresa of Avila makes clear: the Jesus of the flesh is long gone. He is nowhere to be found—neither "sitting at the right hand of God" nor intervening in the affairs of men. His legacy of neighbor love and heart transformation lives on—but only **within you** and **through you** and only if you allow him in.

179

7:37 PM

Mark 12: 28-34 http://www.zeropoint.love

[28]And one of the scholars approached when he heard them arguing, and because he saw how skillfully Jesus answered them, he asked him, "Of all the commandments, which is the most important?" [29]Jesus answered: "The first is, 'Hear, Israel, the Lord your God is one Lord, [30]and you are to

LOVE

the Lord your God with all your heart and all your soul and all your mind and with all your energy.' [31]The second is this: 'You are to **LOVE** your neighbor as yourself.' There is no other commandment greater than these." [32]And the scholar said to him, "That's a fine answer, Teacher. You have correctly said that God is one and there is no other beside him. [33]And 'to **LOVE** him with all one's heart and with all one's mind and with all one's energy' and 'to **LOVE** one's neighbor as oneself' is greater than all the burnt offerings and sacrifices put together." [34]And when Jesus saw that he answered him sensibly, he said to him,

"YOU ARE **NOT FAR** FROM GOD'S DOMAIN."

And from then on no one dared question him.

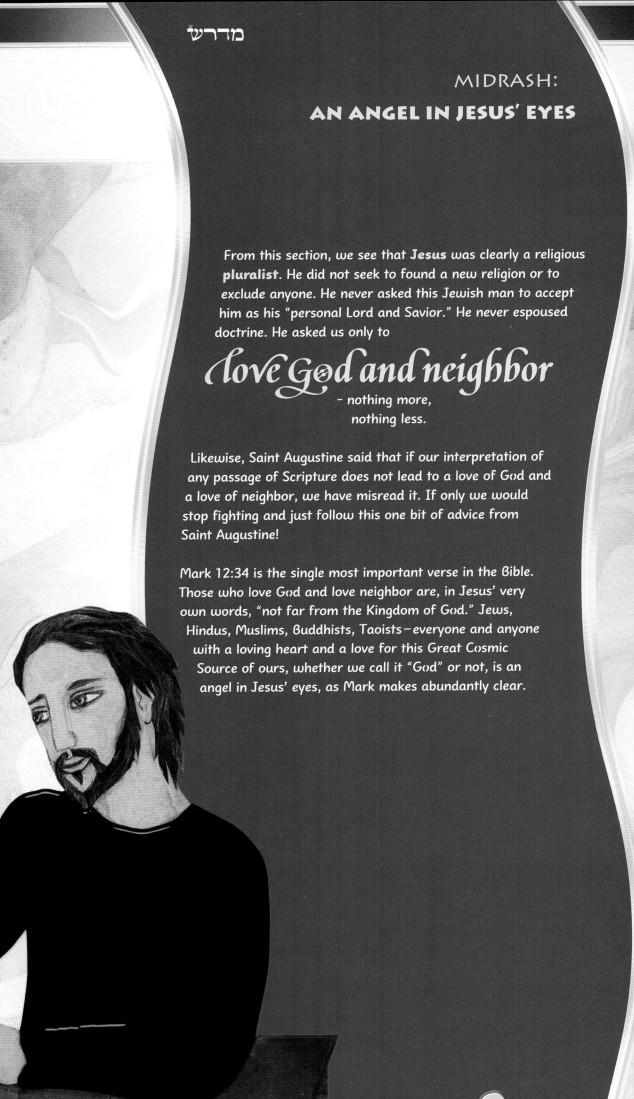

MIDRASH:
AN ANGEL IN JESUS' EYES

From this section, we see that **Jesus** was clearly a religious **pluralist**. He did not seek to found a new religion or to exclude anyone. He never asked this Jewish man to accept him as his "personal Lord and Savior." He never espoused doctrine. He asked us only to

love God and neighbor
- nothing more,
nothing less.

Likewise, Saint Augustine said that if our interpretation of any passage of Scripture does not lead to a love of God and a love of neighbor, we have misread it. If only we would stop fighting and just follow this one bit of advice from Saint Augustine!

Mark 12:34 is the single most important verse in the Bible. Those who love God and love neighbor are, in Jesus' very own words, "not far from the Kingdom of God." Jews, Hindus, Muslims, Buddhists, Taoists—everyone and anyone with a loving heart and a love for this Great Cosmic Source of ours, whether we call it "God" or not, is an angel in Jesus' eyes, as Mark makes abundantly clear.

MIDRASH:

DANCING TOGETHER

"When **Christianity** is seen as **one of the great religions** of the world, as one of the classic forms of the primordial tradition, as a remarkable sacrament of the sacred, it has great credibility. But when Christianity claims to be the only true religion, it loses much of its credibility."
Marcus Borg

"No single tradition monopolizes the truth. We must glean the **best values of all traditions** and work together to remove the tensions between traditions in order to give peace a chance."
Thich Nhat Hanh

"I am a believer in the truth of all great religions of the world. There will be no lasting peace on earth unless we learn not merely to tolerate but even to respect the other faiths as our own. A reverent study of the sayings of different teachers of humanity is a step in the direction of such **mutual respect.**"
Mohandas Gandhi

"In God's family, there are no outsiders. All are insiders. Black and white, rich and poor, gay and straight, Jew and Arab, Palestinian and Israeli, Roman Catholic and Protestant, Serb and Albanian, Hutu and Tutsi, Muslim and Christian, Buddhist and Hindu, Pakistani and Indian—all belong... In our world **we can survive only together.**"
Archbishop Desmond Tutu

In my 36th year,
I came to the heartfelt conclusion that no single tradition
would ever satisfy my

aching spiritual thirst.

I was born and raised
Jewish, and although I am deeply respectful and
appreciative of the faith of my biological ancestors,
I was never entirely satisfied with Judaism alone. I had
a profound born again experience with the Cosmic Christ,
which I described in an early edition of the Gospel of
Matthew. The Cosmic Christ "circumcised my heart," as
the Torah says (Deuteronomy 30:6), and planted an astonishing seed that continues to multiply ten, twenty, even a
hundred times within me. I attended evangelical churches,
poured out my heart at prayer gatherings and weekend
retreats, and walked joyfully in the "body of Christ" for
nearly two years. In the evangelical world—the world of
Spurgeon and Chambers and Fenelon—I soaked in the
radiance of a **Cosmic Spiritual Power** the likes of which
I had never known. No matter the troubles of my life, I
would hold hands with my brothers and sisters in Christ
and pray and give thanks to our Creator. I often quoted
Paul: "Though in tears, always rejoicing; though poor,
enriching others; though having nothing, having everything"
(2 Corinthians 6:10).

But then some of my brethren denounced Catholics and
denied the **primacy of good works**. When I defended the
Catholics and people of other faiths, they accused me of
not being a Christian because I did not believe what they
believed. And then came the war with Iraq; I watched
with shock and embarrassment as all too many Protestant
evangelicals spoke of Islam as "a religion of hate." I
awoke one morning in a cold sweat, terrified and lonely,
feeling as though I was thrust into a lion's den of bigotry
and ignorance. I could take it no longer.

At first, I sought solace in Buddhism, in particular the practice of **Zen meditation** and mantras. Then I discovered the works of Paramahansa Yogananda and fell in love with the Bhagavad Gita and the practice of Yoga, which I now do daily. Then one of the great sayings of the Hindu classic, the Srimad Bhagavatam, really hit me: "Like the bee gathering honey from different flowers, the wise one accepts the essence of different Scriptures and sees only

Good in all religions"
(canto 11, chapter 8, verse 10).

This is it, I decided. Like a bee gathering honey from the flowers of our wisdom traditions, I would forge a beautiful new path. I had discovered my destiny: the Lost Spiritual World series would be a paean to cross pollination, a rapturous affirmation of all that is good and just and honorable in our wisdom traditions.

When someone criticized the great **Vietnamese Buddhist** monk Thich Nhat Hanh's efforts at interfaith dialogue, accusing him of trying to create a fruit salad, he answered, "Fruit salad can be delicious... I do not see any reason to spend one's whole life tasting just one kind of fruit. We human beings can be nourished by the best values of many traditions." I felt a rising tide of joy within me as I discovered writer after writer and guru after guru who embraced not one but many traditions.

"On the altar of my hermitage in France, I have statues of **Buddhas** and **bodhisattvas** and also an image of **Jesus** Christ," says Hanh. "I do not feel any conflict within me. Instead I feel stronger because I have more than one root." I respect the value of being deeply anchored within a tradition; I do not advocate that we create a superficial smorgasbord of faiths. But a smorgasbord need not be superficial; multiple roots strengthen the tree. As Brother David Steindl-Rast notes, there is a difference between being rooted in your faith and being stuck in it.

The **Qur'an** says, "If God had willed it, he could have made you a single nation. But he wanted to create competition among the nations, to see who would **win the prize for good deeds**" (Sura 5.48). What an amazing concept for our war-ravaged, terrorized age! We should indeed compete with one another, says Allah, but not to kill or to conquer, but to do good deeds. And those who do the most good deeds, win. Can there be a more glorious competition than this?

We should not only do good deeds, says the Qur'an, we should "rush to forgive" (Sura 3.133). What a magnificent phrase—

"Rush to forgive!"

Especially in such a stressful world, we regard rushing as undesirable. Yet the one thing that the prophet Muhammad tells us we should rush to do is forgive. Another translation reads, "Race to forgive." Wow! A race to see who can forgive the fastest!

There is so much **beauty in the Qur'an**, just begging for Westerners to discover. Ponder for a moment these wonderfully ecumenical passages: "Be not like those who became divided amongst themselves and have fallen into disagreement" (Sura 3:105). "From the people of Moses, there is a community that leads with truth and establishes justice" (Sura 7.159). "Nearest among them in affection to the believers will you find those who say, 'We are Christians'" (Sura 5:82-83). There is "guidance and light" in the Torah and "guidance and light" in the Gospels (Sura 5:44 and 5:46). "You have your religion and I have mine" (Sura 109).

PENETRATE   DANCE

How many Christians and Jews have reciprocated, saying, "There is guidance and light in the Qur'an, too?" The Qur'an implores people of different religions to "come to common terms" (Sura 3:64). And here is the greatest verse of them all: la ikraha fiddeen, "There is **no compulsion in religion**" (Sura 2:256). Has any prophet of any religion ever uttered a more urgent truth?

The early Church Fathers, likewise, had a Cosmic spirit. They coined a beautiful term, perichoresis, to describe how God the Father, Son and Holy Spirit **interpenetrate** and "**indwell**" in one another. The word was inspired by phrases from the Gospel of John, such as "I am in the Father and the Father is in me" (14:10). Although there is some disagreement about the literal meaning of perichoresis, the theologian Paul Knitter suggests a poetic translation: "dancing together," a kind of intimate spiritual exchange. "The religious traditions of the world can

dance in dialogue

with each other and so grow in both differences and togetherness," writes Knitter. We have already witnessed the beginnings of this **global interpenetration**, this "dancing together" in interfaith charity drives, meetings, seminars, journals and books; with Christians such as Bede Griffiths and Thomas Merton studying Zen meditation; Buddhists such as the Dalai Lama and Thich Nhat Hanh studying the Gospels; Jews such as Rabbi Michael Lerner founding interfaith organizations; and so on.

"By **openness to Buddhism, to Hinduism**, and to these great Asian traditions, we stand a wonderful chance of learning more about the potentiality of our own traditions, because they have gone, from the natural point of view, so much deeper into this than we have," said Thomas Merton.

It is said that there are 84,000 Dharma doors through which we can enter the Buddha's teaching and awakening. Each volume of the Lost Spiritual World series is a little Dharma door, **a search for new manifestations** of the Divine. As Thich Nhat Hanh says, "We should not be afraid of more Dharma doors—if anything, we should be afraid that no more will be opened... Each of us, by our practice and our loving-kindness, is capable of opening new Dharma doors."

And so we search each wisdom tradition, seeking to open new Dharma doors. In the words of Paul, we seek "whatever is true, whatever is honorable, whatever is just, whatever is pure, whatever is pleasing, whatever is commendable" (Phillippians 4:8). Paul is right: **Hinduism** is honorable. **Judaism** is just. **Islam** is pure. **Buddhism** is pleasing. **Christianity** is commendable. We find joy in them all.

As Yogananda says, we can find "a home in the shrines of every faith." Yogananda even liked to spell Krishna as Christna, showing the interconnection of our sages and spiritual traditions.

The writer Raimon Panikkar tells the delightful story of his Catholic mother and Hindu father and how he studied first in America then in India. "I left as a Christian, found myself a Hindu and returned as a Buddhist, without having ceased to be a Christian." Panikkar believes that each wisdom tradition uniquely reveals some aspect of the **Ultimate Mystery** that the other traditions do not. It is a profound distinction: whereas the Rig Veda famously said, "Truth is one; the wise call it by many names" (1.164.46), Panikkar says that each name reveals (or creates) a

different kind of Truth.

RECONCILE   HARMONIZE

If God is infinite, then we **cannot limit God** to one religion. Nor can we limit God to the God of Abraham, as the Buddhists and Hindus do not perceive divinity in this way. In the Hebrew Bible, God speaks through Amos, saying, "People of Israel, I think as much of the Ethiopians as I do of you." In many passages of Torah, God reminds the Jews to be kind to strangers, for they were once strangers in a strange land.

In Zen Buddhism, when you bring your hands together, palm to palm, it is called gassho. The gesture symbolizes the merging of opposites, the collapse of dualities, the harmony and **reconciliation of diverse viewpoints**. We so often mistake this as a "religious" gesture of "piety," not for those who regard themselves as "spiritual, not religious." But it is precisely the kind of gesture we need to make to one another—especially to our enemies.

Our wisdom traditions teach us, above all, to be humble. *"No one knows* its interpretation except God," the Qur'an says of itself (Sura 3:7). Rabbi Marc H. Tanenbaum, one of the pioneers of interfaith dialogue in America, adds, "No one religious, racial, or ethnic group has a monopoly on prejudice or a perfect record of understanding and identifying with the plight of his brothers. All of us need that open-hearted and open-minded process of self-critical examination."

We can be grateful to live in an age in which we can taste the honey of all wisdom traditions. We can be grateful to live in a country in which we can openly and

peacefully express

our love and admiration for each of the Cosmic Prophets, whether Jesus or Buddha or Muhammad or Lao Tzu; openly and peacefully explore commonalities between them; and openly and peacefully meditate with our brothers and sisters of other faiths. As Ken Wilber writes, "We live in an extraordinary time: all the world's cultures, past and present, are to some degree available to us, either in historical records or as living entities. In the history of planet earth, this has never happened before."

Each of us has **a garden inside our hearts**. We can cultivate this garden, deciding, selecting, filtering, pollinating and cross-pollinating. There is nothing more beautiful than a bee buzzing peacefully in God's garden, transforming the ordinary pollen of thought and feeling into a new ambrosia for the human soul.

| Mark 12: 35-44 | | http://www.intention.field ▼ |

[35]And during the time Jesus was teaching in the temple area, he would pose this question: "How can the scholars claim that the Anointed is the son of David? [36]David himself said under the influence of the holy spirit, 'The Lord said to my lord, "Sit here at my right, until I make your enemies grovel at your feet."' [37]David himself calls him 'lord,' so how can he be his son?" And a huge crowd would listen to him with delight. [38]During the course of his teaching he would say: "Look out for the scholars who like to parade around in long robes, and insist on being addressed properly in the marketplaces, [39]and prefer important seats in the synagogues and the best couches at banquets. [40]They are the ones who prey on widows and their families, and recite long prayers just to put on airs. These people will get a stiff sentence!" [41]And he would sit across from the treasury and observe the crowd dropping money into the collection box. And many wealthy people would drop large amounts in. [42]Then one poor widow came and put in two small coins, which is a pittance. [43]And he motioned his disciples over and said to them: "I swear to you, this poor widow has

CONTRIBUTED MORE THAN ALL

those who dropped something into the collection box! [44]After all, they were all donating out of their surplus, whereas she, out of her poverty, was

ALL SHE HAD,

her entire livelihood!"

MIDRASH:

THE SIZE OF YOUR HEART

Though rarely depicted in the history of art, this is one of the most touching moments in all of Mark. Through the heartbreaking coin toss of an impoverished old woman, you can discover a simple

formula for finding God

It is not how much you give but how much of yourself you give that brings you closer to God.

If ever Jesus refuted the Pauline theology of Galatians 2:25 (that we are "justified by faith and not by works"); if ever Jesus made clear that the road to God is through your **good heart** and **good works**—and not through repressive doctrines or empty proclamations of faith—it is in passages such as this. Who knows what this woman believed? Who cares? She found godliness not by talking but by taking action, not by proclaiming her "faith" but by contributing to her community.

This woman had absolutely no faith in Jesus. She likely never even heard of Jesus and she certainly never called him the "Christ." She never read the New Testament. She was never baptized. She was never "saved." And yet, she won the highest praise from Jesus himself, as a **role model** for generations to come.

"It's not the size of your gift, but the size of your heart, that brings you closer to God,"
        says Yogananda.

 BIBLE FACT
Jesus praises this non-Christian woman for her good works and good heart. He never asks her to accept him as her "personal Lord and Savior."

[13]And as he was going out of the temple area, one of his disciples remarks to him, "Teacher, look, what magnificent masonry! What wonderful buildings!" [2]And Jesus replied to him, "Take a good look at these monumental buildings! You may be sure not one stone will be left on top of another! Every last one will certainly be knocked down!" [3]And as he was sitting on the Mount of Olives across from the temple, Peter would ask him privately, as would James and John and Andrew: [4]"Tell us, when are these things going to happen, and what will be the sign to indicate when all these things are about to take place?" [5]And Jesus would say to them, "Stay alert, otherwise someone might just delude you! [6]You know, many will come using my name and claim, 'I'm the one!' and they will delude many people. [7]When you hear of wars and rumors of wars, don't be afraid. These are inevitable, but it is not yet the end. [8]For nation will rise up against nation and empire against empire; there will be earthquakes everywhere; there will be famines. These things mark the beginning of the final agonies. [9]"But you look out for yourselves! They will turn you over to councils, and beat you in synagogues, and haul you up before governors and kings, on my account, so you can make your case to them. [10]Yet the good news must first be announced to all peoples. [11]And when they arrest you to lock you up, don't be worried about what you should say. Instead, whatever occurs to you at the moment, say that. For it is not you who are speaking but the holy spirit. [12]And one brother will turn in another to be put to death, and a father his child, and children will turn against their parents and kill them. [13]And you will be universally hated because of me. Those who hold out to the end will be saved! [14]"When you see the 'devastating desecration' standing where it should not (the reader had better figure out what this means), then the people in Judea should head for the hills; [15]no one on the roof should go downstairs; no one should enter the house to retrieve anything; [16]and no one in the field should turn back to get a coat. [17]It'll be too bad for pregnant women and nursing mothers in those days! [18]Pray that none of this happens in winter! [19]For those days will see distress the likes of which has not occurred since God created the world until now, and will never occur again. [20]And if the Lord had not cut short the days, no human being would have survived! But he did shorten the days for the sake of the chosen people whom he selected. [21]And then if someone says to you, 'Look, here is the Anointed,' or 'Look, there he is!' don't count on it! [22]After all, counterfeit messiahs and phony prophets will show up, and they will provide portents and miracles so as to delude, if possible, even the chosen people. [23]But you be on your guard! Notice how I always warn you about these things in advance. [24]But in those days, after that tribulation, the sun will be darkened, and the moon will not give off her glow, [25]and the stars will fall from the sky, and the heavenly forces will be shaken! [26]"And then they will see the son of Adam coming on the clouds with great power and splendor. [27]And then he will send out messengers and will gather the chosen people from the four winds, from the ends of the earth to the edge of the sky! [28]"Take a cue from the fig tree. When its branch is already in bud and leaves come out, you know that summer is near. [29]So, when you see these things take place, you ought to realize that he is near, just outside your door. [30]I swear to you, this generation certainly won't pass into oblivion before all these things take place! [31]The earth will pass into oblivion and so will the sky, but my words will never be obliterated! [32]"As for that exact day or minute: no one knows, not even heaven's messengers, nor even the son, no one, except the Father. [33]"Be on guard! Stay alert! For you never know what time it is. [34]It's like a person who takes a trip and puts slaves in charge, each with a task, and enjoins the doorkeeper to be alert. [35]Therefore, stay alert! For you never know when the landlord returns, maybe at dusk, or at midnight, or when the rooster crows, or maybe early in the morning. [36]He may return suddenly and find you asleep. [37]What I'm telling you, I say to everyone: Stay alert!"

Mark Chapter 13

In this volume you will find the complete Gospel of Mark, with not a single word added or subtracted. But I cannot lend my heart to Mark 13; I cannot beautify verses of Scripture that continue to be misused by the religious fringes to justify horrific wars, supposedly in the name of a good God and a good-natured Rabbi. The idea that a time of war must precede a time of peace — and that we should do everything we can to hasten the war so we can get to the peace — horrifies us, especially in an age in which nuclear and biochemical annihilation is entirely plausible. Mark's Chapter 13 epitomizes the dangers of interpreting the Bible literally, in a black and white, fundamentalist way.

By giving each individual the right to read the Bible and draw his own heartfelt conclusions, Martin Luther unleashed a seemingly untamable lion inside the Western soul. Your relationship to God is personal, not subject to any human authority. There is great beauty in this idea and I have drawn on it heavily throughout this commentary. But I have been struggling — Luther himself would say "wrestling in the mud" — with a question for which I have no easy answer: do the vocal minority of fundamentalists who seek to hasten Christ's second coming (and destroy Mother Earth in the process) have just as much a right to assert their view of a militant Christ as we do of a peaceful, loving Christ?

For most of my adult life I was a big fan of Luther; but now I am experiencing grave doubts about where he has taken us. The medieval indulgences of the Roman Catholic Church, although abhorrent, seem quaint compared to the crisis of Protestant fundamentalism. In *The Antichrist*, in fact, Nietzsche even apologized for Luther and called the radical strains of Protestantism "indestructible."

In my moments of despair, I recall the words of the Dalai Lama, who said, **"Be the peace that you wish to see in the world."** I acknowledge the crisis of fundamentalism, but I also acknowledge it with peace in my heart. I take a deep breath and recall how my husband and I were stranded on a cold winter night in Boston a few years ago. Our credit cards were maxed out and we could not afford even a cheap hotel. We had only a single sweater between us; it was far too cold and cramped and frightening to park our car somewhere and try to sleep. We made our way to a very affluent neighborhood and knocked on the door of a friend of a friend. At 2:00 a.m., a cherubic, elderly man graciously took us in. My husband lingered with him for a few minutes, though I collapsed on the bed, exhausted; I do not remember having said even a single word.

At breakfast the next morning, the man told us his story. It turns out he had a PhD in engineering from one of the world's top universities and managed a research lab for a technology company. He discovered Christ as a graduate student and in the most gentle, kind-hearted way, began to espouse his fundamentalist beliefs. My husband engaged him in a lively conversation; the enthusiastic vibrations of these two men sent me into deep thought. I savored the delicious home-made pancakes, sipped my coffee and gazed peacefully at the ice crystals formed magically along the roof and the snow-capped pines of the rolling backyard. The words of Matthew 25:35 began to repeat themselves tranquilly in my mind. "I was hungry, and he gave me meat. I was thirsty, and he gave me drink. I was a stranger, and he took me in." Suddenly my eyes flooded with tears. They asked me what was wrong. I said nothing; but in my heart I knew: there were plenty of critics of Christianity in Boston that night, but none of them fed us and none of them took us in.

It was a dreamy, sunny New England day the morning we left, with at least a foot of snow on the ground and not a bird or a plane in the sky, only silence. As my husband pulled out of the driveway, I looked back at the man, who was waving to us gently. His house was worth at least a million dollars, maybe two; but his heart was priceless. On the ride home I could think of nothing but God. There is something deeper in these culture wars, something we all seem to be missing. Maybe fundamentalism, at its best, is not a set of beliefs about God but a set of desires about God. Maybe fundamentalism, at its best, preserves the precious intent of the human heart — to create a common bond between strangers.

I finally understood, at a deep emotional level, what St. John of the Cross meant when he said, "Do not despise others because, as it seems to you, they do not possess virtues you thought they had; they may be pleasing to God for other reasons which you cannot discover." So whenever I cry or feel righteous indignation upon hearing the hurtful and divisive comments of a prominent television fundamentalist, I think immediately of that night in Boston a few years ago and of this man's generous hospitality. I know that millions of wonderful people are attracted to conservative Christianity because they want — as all of us want — to fill the spiritual vacuum in their lives. They want "a purpose driven life" in nurturing, tight-knit communities. And to their credit, they have reminded us how important is the Bible, how much it can still inspire us, and how we ignore it at great peril.

In *Your Best Life Now*, the inspirational pastor Joel Osteen offers a profound technique for dealing with anything we have difficulty understanding (which for many of us includes fundamentalism). We can literally create an "I don't understand it file." We write down what makes no sense to us and file it away. At first, I was skeptical that this would have any positive impact on my life; but I noticed something magical started to happen the moment I filed away my inner troubles. Most often, they just disappeared.

Mark's Chapter 13 is not Christian prophecy but a rehash of ancient Jewish eschatology, which the Jews themselves later rejected. We, too, can reject it. And the best way to reject it is not through war or anger but gratitude; for it is not possible to be angry and grateful at the same time. We can be grateful for the many wonderful people of all faiths and the many beautiful passages of the Scriptures of all traditions that could lead — if enough of us share the dream — to peace on earth. In Luke 17:21, Jesus says, "The Kingdom of heaven is within you." In English, "you" is often misunderstood as a singular pronoun, suggesting that each of us, alone, can find a Heaven within ourselves. But the original Greek is plural, suggesting that we find Heaven only by working together. A more accurate translation is, "The Kingdom of Heaven is in your midst." If the Kingdom is truly in our midst, then we need not hasten wars or tribulations. The Good News of the Cosmic Christ is not that the final days are coming but that by the love and grace of God they need not come.

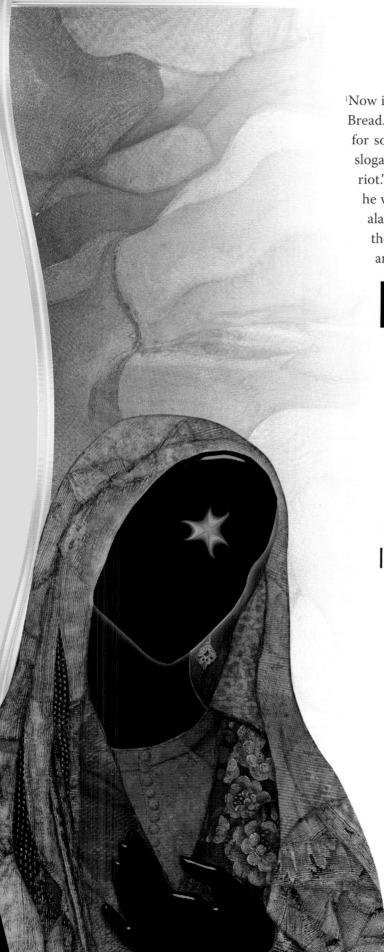

[1]Now it was two days until Passover and the feast of Unleavened Bread. And the ranking priests and the scholars were looking for some way to arrest him by trickery and kill him. [2]For their slogan was: "Not during the festival, otherwise the people will riot." [3]When he was in Bethany at the house of Simon the leper, he was just reclining there, and a woman came in carrying an alabaster jar of myrrh, of pure and expensive nard. She broke the jar and poured (the myrrh) on his head. [4]Now some were annoyed (and thought) to themselves: "What good

PURPOSE

is served by this waste of myrrh? [5]For she could have sold the myrrh for more than three hundred silver coins and given (the money) to the poor." And they were angry with her. [6]Then Jesus said, "Let her alone! Why are you bothering her? She has done me a courtesy. [7]Remember, there will always be poor around, and whenever you want you can do good for them, but I won't always be around. [8]She did what she could— she anticipates in anointing my body for burial. [9]So help me, wherever the good news is announced in all the world, what she has done will also be told

IN MEMORY OF **HER!**"

MIDRASH:

A HUMBLE HEROINE

Here is one of the most beautiful and visionary scenes in the entire Bible. An **anonymous woman** pours the anointing oil on Jesus, as prophesied in Exodus 30:25 and 1 Samuel 10:1. The oil would have been called the shemen hamish-kah, literally the "Messiah oil," though Mark may have been unfamiliar with the term. The scene is remarkable for several reasons: first that a woman is doing the anointing, something unheard of in ancient times. Second, although the woman was likely **Mary Magdalene**, as Bruce Chilton suggests, Mark never names her despite naming many men of lesser consequence in the story.

Between the lines of Mark's Gospel we glean an archetype of great beauty, a

visionary yet humble

heroine who resonates especially for us. Two thousand years later, her anonymity does not stop us from remembering her, just as Jesus predicted. No matter our status in life, no matter our level of fame or recognition, no matter how much those in power try to marginalize us, we each have an important contribution to make.

In **WomanWord**, a magnificent book of prayers in honor of the great women of the Bible, Sister Miriam Therese Winter interprets this scene for men and women of all ages:

Anoint my hands to hold and heal
 the many lives that are broken,
  that I may do good,
   do what I must
    to bring hope into hopelessness.

¹⁰And Judas Iscariot, one of the twelve, went off to the ranking priests to turn him over to them. ¹¹When they heard, they were delighted, and promised to pay him in silver. And he started looking for some way to turn him in at the right moment. ¹²On the first day of Unleavened Bread, when they would sacrifice the Passover lamb, his disciples say to him, "Where do you want us to go and get things ready for you to

CELEBRATE

Passover?" ¹³He sends two of his disciples and says to them, "Go into the city, and someone carrying a waterpot will meet you. Follow him, ¹⁴and whatever place he enters say to the head of the house, 'The teacher asks, "Where is my guest room where I can

CELEBRATE

Passover with my disciples?"' ¹⁵And he'll show you a large upstairs room that has been arranged. That's the place you're to get ready for us."

http://www.lostspiritualworld.com   **Mark 14: 17-26**

[16]And the disciples left, went into the city, and found it exactly as he had told them; and they got things ready for Passover. [17]When evening comes, he arrives with the twelve. [18]And as they reclined at table and were eating, Jesus said, "So help me, one of you eating with me is going to turn me in!" [19]They began to fret and to say to him one after another, "I'm not the one, am I?" [20]But he said to them, "It's one of the twelve, the one who is dipping into the bowl with me. [21]The son of Adam departs just as the scriptures predict, but damn the one responsible for turning the son of Adam in! It would be better for that man had he never been born!" [22]And as they were eating, he took a loaf, gave a blessing, broke it into pieces and offered it to them. And he said, "Take some; this is my body!" [23]He also took a cup, gave thanks, and offered it to them, and they all drank from it. [24]And he said to them: "This is my blood of the covenant, which has been poured out for many! [25]So help me, I certainly won't drink any of the fruit of the vine again until that day when I drink it for the first time in God's domain!" [26]And they

SANG A HYMN

and left for the Mount of Olives.

[27]And Jesus says to them, "You will all lose faith. Remember, scripture says, 'I will strike the shepherd and the sheep will be scattered!' [28]But after I'm raised I'll go ahead of you to Galilee." [29]Peter said to him, "Even if everyone else loses faith, I won't!" [30]And Jesus says to him, "So help me, tonight before the rooster crows twice you will disown me three times!" [31]But he repeated it with more bluster: "If they condemn me to die with you, I will never disown you!" And they took the same oath — all of them. [32]And they go to a place the name of which was Geth sem ane, and he says to his disciples, "Sit down here while I pray." [33]And he takes Peter and James and John along with him, and he grew apprehensive and full of anguish. [34]He says to them,

"I'M SO SAD I COULD DIE.

You stay here and be alert!" [35]And he would move on a little, fall on the ground, and pray that he might avoid the crisis, if possible.

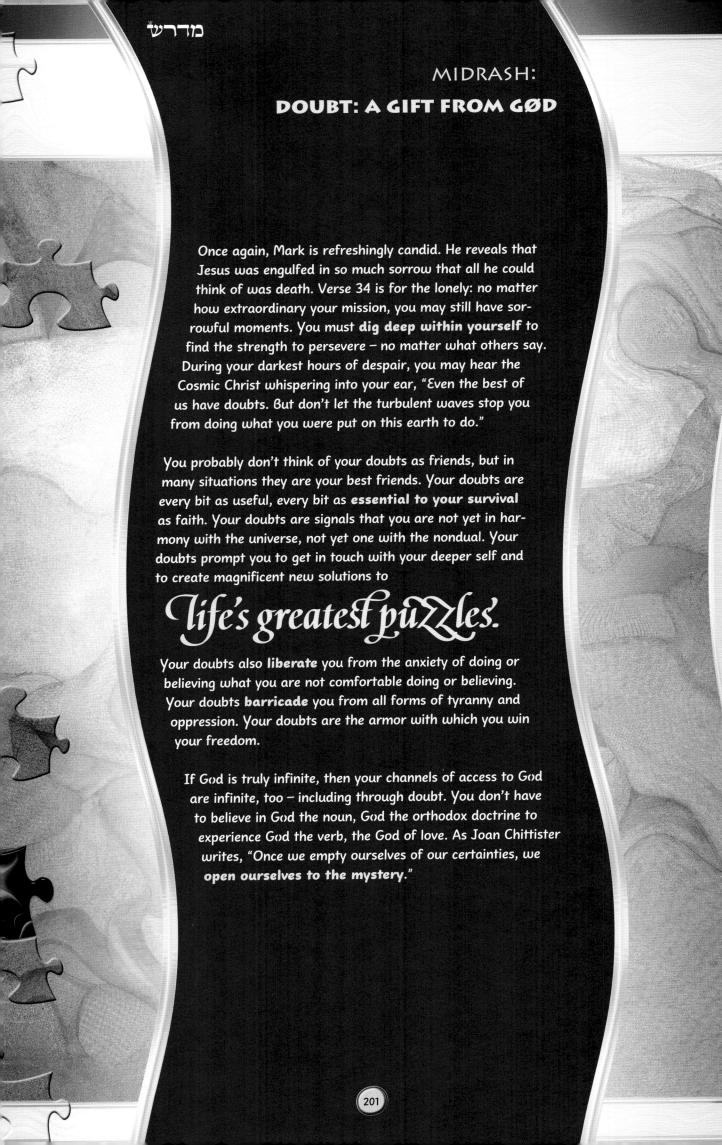

MIDRASH:

DOUBT: A GIFT FROM GØD

Once again, Mark is refreshingly candid. He reveals that Jesus was engulfed in so much sorrow that all he could think of was death. Verse 34 is for the lonely: no matter how extraordinary your mission, you may still have sorrowful moments. You must **dig deep within yourself** to find the strength to persevere – no matter what others say. During your darkest hours of despair, you may hear the Cosmic Christ whispering into your ear, "Even the best of us have doubts. But don't let the turbulent waves stop you from doing what you were put on this earth to do."

You probably don't think of your doubts as friends, but in many situations they are your best friends. Your doubts are every bit as useful, every bit as **essential to your survival** as faith. Your doubts are signals that you are not yet in harmony with the universe, not yet one with the nondual. Your doubts prompt you to get in touch with your deeper self and to create magnificent new solutions to

life's greatest puzzles.

Your doubts also **liberate** you from the anxiety of doing or believing what you are not comfortable doing or believing. Your doubts **barricade** you from all forms of tyranny and oppression. Your doubts are the armor with which you win your freedom.

If God is truly infinite, then your channels of access to God are infinite, too – including through doubt. You don't have to believe in God the noun, God the orthodox doctrine to experience God the verb, the God of love. As Joan Chittister writes, "Once we empty ourselves of our certainties, we **open ourselves to the mystery.**"

Mark 14: 36-42 http://www.connection.cosmic

[36]And he would say,

"ABBA (Father),

ALL THINGS ARE

POSSIBLE

for you! Take this cup away from me! But it's not what I want (that matters), but what you want." [37]And he returns and finds them sleeping, and says to Peter, "Simon, are you sleeping? Couldn't you stay awake for one hour? [38]Be alert and pray that you won't be put to the test! Though the spirit is willing, the flesh is weak." [39]And once again he went away and prayed, saying the same thing. [40]And once again he came and found them sleeping, since their eyes had grown very heavy, and they didn't know what to say to him. [41]And he comes a third time and says to them, "You may as well sleep on now and get your rest. It's all over! The time has come! Look, the son of Adam is being turned over to foreigners. [42]Get up, let's go! See for yourselves! Here comes the one who is going to turn me in."

MIDRASH:

CALLING GOD "POP"

In the Hebrew Scriptures, man's relationship to God is often **distant** and **terrifying**. When Moses ascended Mount Sinai to receive the Ten Commandments, the Jews "trembled in fear and stayed at a distance" (Exodus 20:18). Moses himself had to turn away from the burning bush, "for he was afraid to look at God" (Exodus 3:6).

Abba is Aramaic for father, but it is a very warm and affectionate word, similar to "**Pop**." No Jewish prophet—not even Moses—would have dared call God his "Abba." He was not even permitted to write the name of God. So when Rabbi Jesus called God his Abba, he introduced a new kind of

Cosmic Spirituality.

Calling God his Abba was Jesus' way of saying: from now on, our relationship to the Cosmos is **personal**.

Father Tielhard de Chardin, a prophet for our times, illuminated this spiritual concept in a profoundly new way. Chardin made three important distinctions: "Energy-as-God" (what many skeptics and nonbelievers call it); "Thinking Energy as God"; and "Thinking Energy as God the Transcendent Personality," e.g. the "Cosmic Christ" or the "Cosmic Abba." This is the core of Chardin's brilliance: in the quantum universe that is shaped as much by the light within as without, **you can shape it** in one of three ways. You can say that God is energy, that God is thinking Energy, or that Energy and Thinking Energy are two aspects of something far more magnificent: **a personal relationship** with this Quantum Energy. You can think of it coldly, as an "it"; or you can think of it warmly, as "Abba" (or "Thou" as Buber called it). And if the quantum physics of our day allows us this choice, who would want to think of the Universe as a mere it?

Chardin explored how religion is still growing and evolving, just as Science is still growing and evolving. Science makes you aware of the immensity of the cosmos; religion makes you aware of the immensity of the cosmos within. Our new Cosmic Consciousness can be

ʃuniquely ʃersonal,

derived from and inspired by the archetype of Christ and of Abba, because Christianity approaches spirituality in a uniquely personal way.

"Who knows what astonishing species and natural gradations of soul are even now being produced by the persevering efforts of Science?" asked Chardin, himself a respected paleontologist. "Even those who do not believe sense and see through the magic immensities of the cosmos."

If you could choose to be alive in any time in history, which would you choose? The medieval cosmology of superstition, of a flat world with the sun revolving around the earth? The cold, mechanistic, Newtonian view of a universe that struts and frets like clockwork? Or the emerging,

warm worldview

of today, which reveres the beauty and rarity of every breath you take and every heart you touch?

The renowned cosmologist Joel Primack is one of the pioneers of the "cold dark matter" theory. He and his wife Nancy Abrams stand on the spiritual shoulders of Chardin and Buber, but their perspective is vastly enriched by the most recent scientific discoveries. Their book, **The View from the Center of the Universe,** offers a profound meditation on the centrality of man and womankind within the cosmos.

"By the spiritual we mean the relationship between a conscious mind and the cosmos," they write. "The faith of active research cosmologists—a faith shared with the ancients—is that human beings can **personally connect** in a meaningful way to the real cosmos." The language of Abrams and Primack is surprising, even astonishing, given their scientific credentials. They use words like "relationship" and "choice" and phrases like "personally connect" to describe the new cosmological paradigm that has emerged from the Hubble telescope and other scientific instruments.

Along with writers such as Thomas Berry and cosmologists such as Brian Swimme, Primack and Abrams are helping to reimagine our world through new metaphors. They explore the profound implications of our bodies being made mostly of stardust. They refer to hydrogen and helium as our **cosmic ancestors**—in some profound way, our grandparents. "There may be no better way to compress the untold ages of time between ourselves and the beginning —emphasizing the enduring, personal relationship across that immense gap—than to think of those **original creative forces** as 'grandparents.'"

One of the most powerful ideas of Primack and Abrams —an idea whose spiritual implications we are yet to digest —is that God himself is expanding. "The more that people discover about the universe," they write, "the faster

God keeps expanding,
always ahead,
pulling yet teasing scientists... In this way scientific discoveries endlessly enrich the possibilities of God."

God, in other words, is a magnificent work in progress.

You are on a flying space ship—Earth—in a flying galaxy—the Milky Way—in a rapidly expanding universe whose reach far exceeds your grasp. Here you are, in a blissful break from eternity, to contemplate it all.

The Book of Genesis was right: from dust we came — stardust. And now the dust of stars is the

dust of a new dream,

of humanity transformed and at peace, evolving as the Universe evolves and expanding as God expands.

Andrew Cohen, editor of the spiritual magazine, **What Is Enlightenment?** writes, "The universe, as far as we know, is only just beginning to become conscious of itself, through us. That is why the ultimate point and purpose of the whole ordeal of evolution, and finally of enlightenment itself, could not be merely the transcendence of or escape from the world, but rather the active transformation or enlightenment of the world."

We are living at the dawn of a new axial age, with the old religions responding to Science with a new paradigm, a new way of understanding ourselves. Abba puts a spiritual face on that which we can neither define nor comprehend. By meditating, sharing, helping, giving and affirming the goodness of the Cosmic Abba, we participate in a **deeply personal form of spirituality**—a spirituality that transcends ordinary human awareness and that fills us with awe and gratitude for everything within and without.

http://www.lostspiritualworld.com **Mark 14: 36**

" We are in the midst of a revelatory experience of the Universe that compares in magnitude to those of the great religious revelations. We need only wander about, telling the Great Story to ignite a Transformation of humanity."

Michael Dowd

 Your spiritual network is now connected

Connected to: The Cosmos
Signal Strength: Very Good

[43]And right away, while he was still speaking, Judas, one of the twelve, shows up, and with him a crowd, dispatched by the ranking priests and the scholars and the elders, wielding swords and clubs. [44]Now the one who was to turn him in had arranged a signal with them, saying, "The one I'm going to kiss is the one you want. Arrest him and escort him safely away!" [45]And right away he arrives, comes up to him, and says, "Rabbi," and kissed him. [46]And they seized him and held him fast. [47]One of those standing around drew his sword and struck the high priest's slave and cut off his ear. [48]In response Jesus said to them, "Have you come out to take me with swords and clubs as though you were apprehending a rebel? [49]I was with you in the temple area day after day teaching and you didn't lift a hand against me. But the scriptures must come true!"

[50] AND THEY **ALL DESERTED** HIM AND **RAN AWAY.**

[51]And a young man was following him, wearing a shroud over his nude body, and they grab him. [52]But he dropped the shroud and ran away naked. [53]And they brought Jesus before the high priest, and all the ranking priests and elders and scholars assemble. [54]Peter followed him at a distance until he was inside the courtyard of the high priest, and was sitting with the attendants and keeping warm by the fire. [55]The ranking priests and the whole Council were looking for evidence against Jesus in order to issue a death sentence, but they couldn't find any. [56]Although many gave false evidence against him, their stories didn't agree. [57]And some people stood up and testified falsely against him: [58]"We have heard him saying, 'I'll destroy this temple made with hands and in three days I'll build another, not made with hands!'" [59]Yet even then their stories did not agree.

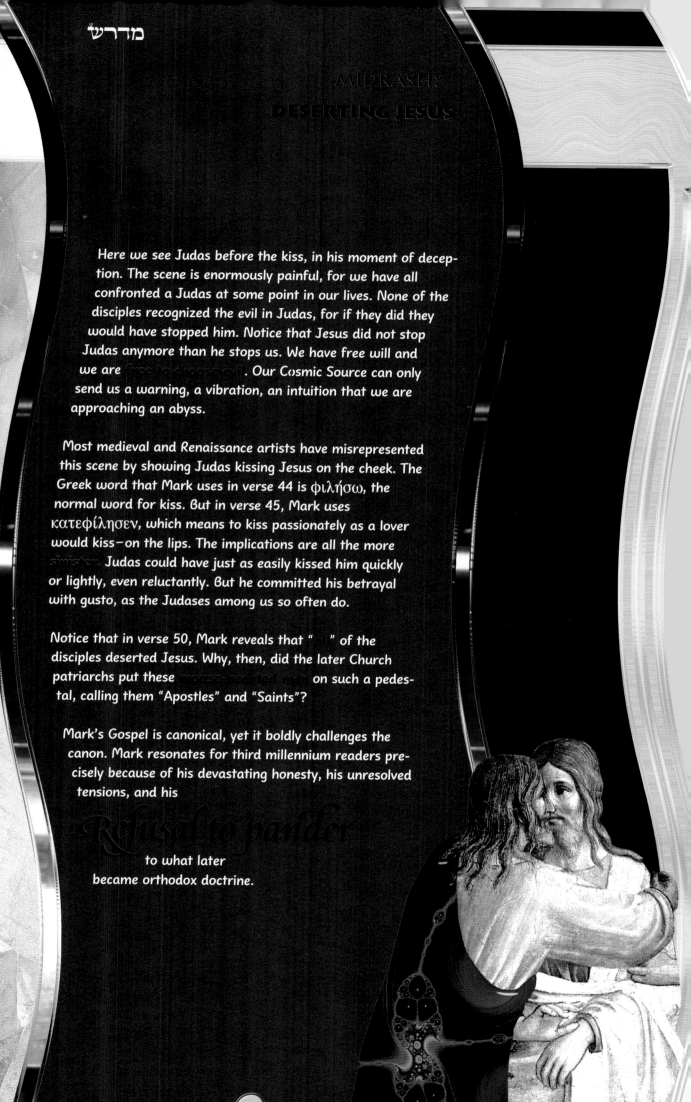

Here we see Judas before the kiss, in his moment of deception. The scene is enormously painful, for we have all confronted a Judas at some point in our lives. None of the disciples recognized the evil in Judas, for if they did they would have stopped him. Notice that Jesus did not stop Judas anymore than he stops us. We have free will and we are free to choose evil. Our Cosmic Source can only send us a warning, a vibration, an intuition that we are approaching an abyss.

Most medieval and Renaissance artists have misrepresented this scene by showing Judas kissing Jesus on the cheek. The Greek word that Mark uses in verse 44 is φιλήσω, the normal word for kiss. But in verse 45, Mark uses κατεφίλησεν, which means to kiss passionately as a lover would kiss—on the lips. The implications are all the more sinister. Judas could have just as easily kissed him quickly or lightly, even reluctantly. But he committed his betrayal with gusto, as the Judases among us so often do.

Notice that in verse 50, Mark reveals that "all" of the disciples deserted Jesus. Why, then, did the later Church patriarchs put these mouse-hearted men on such a pedestal, calling them "Apostles" and "Saints"?

Mark's Gospel is canonical, yet it boldly challenges the canon. Mark resonates for third millennium readers precisely because of his devastating honesty, his unresolved tensions, and his

Refusal to pander

to what later
became orthodox doctrine.

MIDRASH: DENYING JESUS

How many times do we want to

Speak the Truth,

intend to speak the truth, and yet, in a weak moment, find ourselves frightened and unprepared—and blurt out an untruth? We are often surprised, sometimes even shocked, by the words that escape from our lips, seemingly beyond our control. Peter suffered from such moments —and from remorse, too.

Consider the reverse of Peter: someone who proclaims Jesus Christ with his lips—parades around saying that Jesus Christ is his "personal Lord and Savior"—but does not love his neighbor (or even people of other faiths and other views) with all his heart. One of the great lessons of Peter's denial is that what proceeds from the lips does not always reflect what proceeds from the heart. Our lips are a poor barometer of how much we love God.

Peter was a weak, fearful, and mouse-hearted man who "cursed," "swore," "denied," and "disowned." It is difficult to imagine a more flawed founder of the Christian Church. Yet we find inspiration in Peter's story because Jesus still loved him and still gave him the awesome responsibility of perpetuating his legacy. Likewise, your Sacred Source still loves you, even when your lips disappoint. You have a destiny to fulfill. You can never let your shortcomings stop you.

⁶⁰And the high priest got up and questioned Jesus: "Don't you have some answer to give? Why do these people testify against you?" ⁶¹But he was silent and refused to answer. Once again the high priest questioned him and says to him, "Are you the Anointed, the son of the Blessed One?" ⁶²Jesus replied, "I am! And you will see the son of Adam sitting at the right hand of Power and coming with the clouds of the sky!" ⁶³Then the high priest tore his vestments and says, "Why do we still need witnesses? ⁶⁴You have heard the blasphemy! What do you think?" And they all concurred in the death penalty. ⁶⁵And some began to spit on him, and to put a blindfold on him, and punch him, and say to him, "Prophesy!" And the guards abused him as they took him into custody. ⁶⁶And while Peter was below in the courtyard, one of the high priest's slave women comes over, ⁶⁷and sees Peter warming himself; she looks at him closely, then speaks up: "You too were with that Nazarene, Jesus!" ⁶⁸But he

DENIED

it, saying, "I haven't the slightest idea what you're talking about!" And he went outside into the forecourt. ⁶⁹And when the slave woman saw him, she once again began to say to those standing nearby, "This fellow is one of them!" ⁷⁰But once again he **DENIED** it. And a little later, those standing nearby would again say to Peter, "You really are one of them, since you also are a Galilean!" ⁷¹But he began to **CURSE** and **SWEAR**, "I don't know the fellow you're talking about!" ⁷²And just then a rooster crowed a second time, and Peter remembered what Jesus had told him: "Before a rooster crows twice you will **DISOWN** me three times!" And he broke down and started to cry.

Mark 15: 1-15   http://www.darkenergy.blog

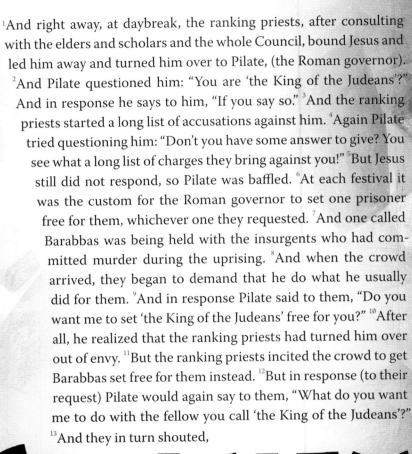

[1]And right away, at daybreak, the ranking priests, after consulting with the elders and scholars and the whole Council, bound Jesus and led him away and turned him over to Pilate, (the Roman governor). [2]And Pilate questioned him: "You are 'the King of the Judeans'?" And in response he says to him, "If you say so." [3]And the ranking priests started a long list of accusations against him. [4]Again Pilate tried questioning him: "Don't you have some answer to give? You see what a long list of charges they bring against you!" [5]But Jesus still did not respond, so Pilate was baffled. [6]At each festival it was the custom for the Roman governor to set one prisoner free for them, whichever one they requested. [7]And one called Barabbas was being held with the insurgents who had committed murder during the uprising. [8]And when the crowd arrived, they began to demand that he do what he usually did for them. [9]And in response Pilate said to them, "Do you want me to set 'the King of the Judeans' free for you?" [10]After all, he realized that the ranking priests had turned him over out of envy. [11]But the ranking priests incited the crowd to get Barabbas set free for them instead. [12]But in response (to their request) Pilate would again say to them, "What do you want me to do with the fellow you call 'the King of the Judeans'?" [13]And they in turn shouted,

"CRUCIFY

him!" [14]Pilate kept saying to them, "Why? What has he done wrong?" But they shouted all the louder,

"CRUCIFY

him!" [15]And because Pilate was always looking to satisfy the crowd, he set Barabbas free for them, had Jesus flogged, and then turned him over to be crucified.

This mob scene has played itself out countless thousands of times throughout history: the Salem witch trials, the burnings at the stake of Tyndale and Bruno, the lynching of black men after the American Civil War by white Christians, often in the name of Christ. Bosch did not have to look far for inspiration for his macabre portrayal of Jesus' final walk. The great historian Gibbons once said, "History is little more than a register of the crimes, follies and misfortunes of man." The deeper lesson is that we should be about our own capacity to recognize greatness, appreciate beauty or avoid catastrophe. Our   the odd genius or visionary prophet—whether literally or in blogs—is an all too familiar affair. One wonders whether this lust is biologically ingrained.

Just as our love of God connects us to people of earlier millenniums, so does our lust to lynch. We are the most advanced culture in history, but hardly the kindest. We have more knowledge, but

We still judge others
and so history still judges us.

MIDRASH:
WHY IS THIS "GOOD NEWS"?

Throughout Mark's Gospel, we read of the Jewish disciples'
confusion and shock at the crucifixion. In Mark 8:32,

Peter "Rebuked" Jesus,

(as the NIV words it) for thinking he needed to be crucified
before his message would be heard. Two thousand years
later, we still share Peter's heartache. That God would
allow his "favored son" to be crucified is a strange, even
perverse notion. Must a prophet suffer and die upon
a cross before his message can impact the world? Why?
Were his teachings not enough? Could we not throw out
the Passion cycle and still embrace the ideals of the Cosmic
Christ? Many of us still agree with Paul, who wrote, "The
crucifixion is repulsive to the Jews and foolish to the
Gentiles" (1 Corinthians 1:23).

It is surprising to discover how deeply rooted in Jewish and
Egyptian literature was the Passion cycle. If we combine four
Jewish texts—Isaiah 53, Psalms 22 & 69, and the Wisdom of
Solomon 2—we get an almost verbatim account of Mark's
Passion cycle. Long before Mark, the Egyptians told of Osiris,
likewise a "son of God" who was crucified and rose from
the dead after three days. Perhaps because he borrowed
so much and embellished so little, Mark leaves us deeply
unsatisfied. In both past and present tense, three times
in three verses, Mark tells us: "And they crucify. And they
crucified. And they crucify." OK, so they crucified. But then
what? All Jesus could do in his dying breath was cry out to
God, "Why have you abandoned me?" Then he died. Why is
this Good News? Why is Mark so excited? What is redemp-
tive in this?

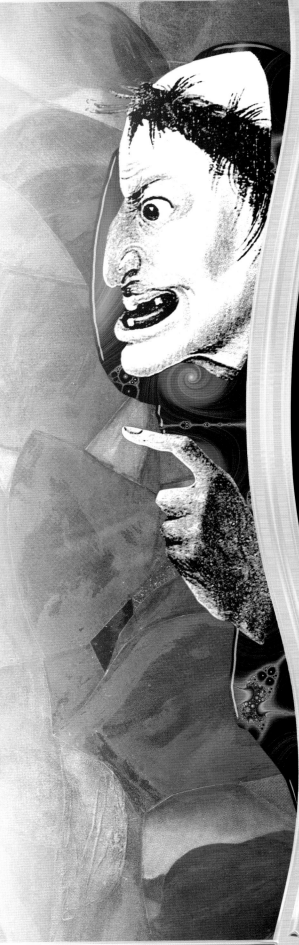

[16]And the Roman soldiers led him away to the courtyard of the governor's residence, and they called the whole company (of Roman troops) together. [17]And they dressed him in purple and crowned him with a garland woven of thorns. [18]And the soldiers began to salute him: "Greetings, 'King of the Judeans'!" [19]And they kept striking him on the head with a staff, and **SPITTING** on him; and they would get down on their knees and bow down to him. [20]And when they had **MADE FUN OF HIM**, they stripped off the purple and put his own clothes back on him. And the Romans lead him out to **CRUCIFY HIM**. [21]And they conscript someone named Simon of Cyrene, who was coming in from the country, the father of Alexander and Rufus, to carry his cross. [22]And the Roman soldiers bring him to the place Golgotha (which means "Place of the Skull"). [23]And they tried to give him wine mixed with myrrh, but he didn't take it. [24]And the soldiers **CRUCIFY HIM**, and they divide up his garments, casting lots to see who would get what. [25]It was nine o'clock in the morning when they **CRUCIFIED HIM**. [26]And the inscription, which identified his crime, read, 'The King of the Judeans.' [27]And with him they **CRUCIFY** two rebels, one on his right and one on his left. [28,29]Those passing by kept **TAUNTING** him, **WAGGING** their heads, and saying, "Ha! You who would destroy the temple and rebuild it in three days, [30]save yourself and come down from the cross!" [31]Likewise the ranking priests had **MADE FUN OF HIM** to one another, along with the scholars; they would say, "He saved others, but he can't save himself! [32]'The Anointed,' 'the King of Israel,' should come down from the cross here and now, so that we can see and trust for ourselves!" Even those being **CRUCIFIED** along with him would

ABUSE

him.

Mark 15: 33-39 http://www.crucifixion.spirit

³³And when noon came, darkness blanketed the whole land until mid-afternoon. ³⁴And at 3 o'clock in the afternoon Jesus shouted at the top of his voice, "Eloi, Eloi, lema sabachthani" (which means

"MY GOD, MY GOD, **WHY** DID YOU ABANDON

me?"). ³⁵And when some of those standing nearby heard, they would say, "Listen, he's calling Elijah!" ³⁶And someone ran and filled a sponge with sour wine, stuck it on a pole, and offered him a drink, saying, "Let's see if Elijah comes to rescue him!" ³⁷But Jesus let out a great shout and breathed his last. ³⁸And the curtain of the temple was torn in two from top to bottom! ³⁹When the Roman officer standing opposite him saw that he had died like this, he said, "This man really was God's son!"

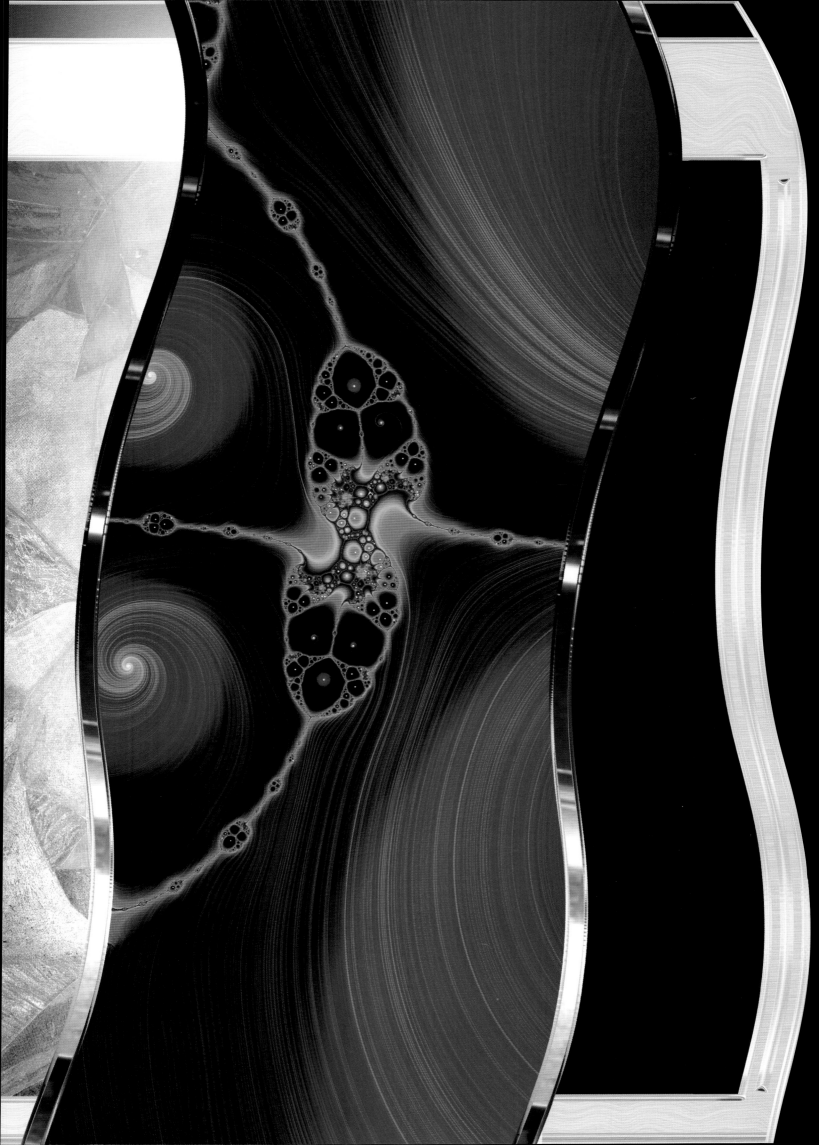

[40]Now some

WOMEN

were observing this from a distance, among whom were Mary of Magdala, and Mary the mother of James the younger and Joses, and Salome. [41](These women) had

REGULARLY

FOLLOWED AND ASSISTED

him when he was in Galilee, along with

MANY OTHER WOMEN

who had come up to Jerusalem in his company. [42]And when it had already grown dark, since it was preparation day (the day before the sabbath), [43]Joseph of Arimathea, a respected council member, who himself was anticipating God's imperial rule, appeared on the scene, and dared to go to Pilate to request the body of Jesus. [44]And Pilate was surprised that he had died so soon. He summoned the Roman officer and asked him whether he had been dead for long. [45]And when he had been briefed by the Roman officer, he granted the body to Joseph. [46]And he bought a shroud and took him down and wrapped him in the shroud, and placed him in a tomb that had been hewn out of rock, and rolled a stone up against the opening of the tomb. [47]And Mary of Magdala and Mary the mother of Joses noted where he had been laid to rest.

MIDRASH:

SPIRIT CRUCIFIED

"When God is male, the male is God." Mary Daly

In the drama of the crucifixion, we tend to overlook a remarkable detail preserved by Mark but minimized or even eliminated by the later Gospel writers. In Mark 15:41, we learn that **women** "had regularly followed and assisted (Jesus) when he was in Galilee, along with many other women who had come up to Jerusalem in his company." Indeed, we have seen how women served Jesus throughout Mark's Gospel, from 1:31 to 14:3. Jesus himself said, "Whoever wants to become great must be your servant" (Mark 10:43). The

heart of Christianity
is service; Mark's Gospel

makes clear that women were the **servants**, **followers**, **companions**, **helpers** and true **disciples of Jesus**. The women were the embodiment of Christian devotion; but as we have seen repeatedly (6:3, 6:6, 6:37, 6:52, 8:33, 10:13, 10:26, 10:28, 10:37, 14:37, 14:68), the men were often doubtful, hesitant, obstinate, conniving and selfish.

The issues extend far beyond the historical facts. Linguists from Ludwig Wittgenstein to Noam Chomsky to Steven Pinker have made us profoundly aware of how language structures our perception of the world, including gender. A number of important Biblical words are **feminine**, such as rachamim, which means **compassion**; hokhmah, which means **wisdom**; and ruach, which means Spirit. A famous line from the earliest surviving fragments of the Gospel of the Hebrews reads, "Just now my Mother, the Holy Spirit, took me by one of my hairs and brought me to Tabor, the great mountain." Origen and Jerome, the Church fathers, cited this verse with fascination and respect. The Syrian Church of the second and third centuries even worshiped **"Our Mother, the Holy Spirit"**; they did not worship our Father, the Holy Spirit. Jesus himself says, "My true Mother gave me life" (Gospel of Thomas 101). Not the father.

The Gospel of Philip (55:24) ridicules the idea of the virgin birth—not for any supernatural absurdity, but for its gender impossibility. "Some said, 'Mary conceived by the holy spirit.' They are in error. They do not know what they are saying. When did a woman ever conceive by a woman?"

The Gospels of Philip and Thomas were bitterly opposed —and ultimately suppressed—as the Christian Testament was canonized by an entirely male group of non-Jewish Christians two centuries later. When Constantine made Christianity the official religion of Rome, he transformed its Church into a bastion of male power. His bishops laid down rules and invented laws, contrary to the teachings of Mary's Gospel (10:13). They also invented or aggrandized a number of critical verses in the New Testament to rationalize their subordination of women, such as:

"Man is the head of every woman" (1 Corinthians 11:3). "Women should be silent in the churches, for they are not permitted to speak, but should be submissive" (1 Corinthians 14:33). "Wives, submit to your own husbands as to the Lord, for the husband is the head" (Ephesians 5:21). "I do not allow a woman to teach or to have authority over a man; instead, she is to be silent" (1 Timothy 2:12). Notice that all of these verses come from later Christian writings and

None are from Jesus.

They are quoted to this day in tens of thousands of (Pauline) churches to justify the continued subordination and oppression of women worldwide.

A recent study by Duke Divinity School found that "not a single woman was mentioned by conservative Protestants" on their reading lists. Even in this year of our Transformer, 2006, conservative Protestants still refuse to read some of the **finest Christian commentators of any generation,** among them Elaine Pagels, Karen Armstrong, Miriam Therese Winter, Karen King, Joan Chittister and Diana Eck—simply because they are women. When a man writes a book of theology, he is described as a "theologian." But when a woman writes a book of theology, she is still described as a "feminist theologian." One major review publication recently described Elizabeth Schuessler Fiorenza—who is indisputably one of the most important theologians of our time, male or female—as "the radical feminist theologian." Despite great strides, women are still "radically other" in many parts of the world, still marginalized, still crucified as second fiddle.

The continued refusal of numerous Catholic and Protestant leaders to afford women equal rights and equal responsibilities within the church (let alone to read their books) bespeaks a tragic lack of **humility**. If history has taught us anything—better said, if history has proven anything beyond a shadow of a doubt—it is that far too many men have made a mockery of the **genuine**, **heartfelt**, **compassionate** teachings of Jesus the Christ.

Sister Joan Chittister keenly observes, "**Women's peacemaking** is, without doubt, different from the peace processes followed by men. Women reach out to one another, to their children, to the personal needs of the people around them. Women do not seek to win a conflict. They seek to stop it. The world has a great deal to learn from the way

Women break through

present fears and old resentments more readily, more openly than, history tells us, do the (mostly) male leaders who make peace at the end of a gun, who treat peacemaking as a matter of reaching formal agreements which, when they fail, only justify going to war again."

The crucifixion isn't just a story or a fairy tale. It's about us. It's about who we are as a species. It's about the shortcomings, cruelties and injustices that persist to this day. The genderless Cosmic Christ (Mark 12:25) calls us to action, to commit ourselves to **social justice** and transcendent healing. he inspires us to do more than simply heal ourselves in some narrow, narcissistic way; he asks us to heal by reaching out to others and standing up for the oppressed—male and female.

The last thing the world needs is another portrait of a man on the cross. "Spirit Crucified" cries out in defiance of the "great" religious art of the past, which is based upon a strain of orthodox Christian doctrine that no longer serves us. The "great" male artists who portrayed a highly Romanized, non-Jewish male figure on the cross have pulled quite a ruse on the Western mind: the man suffers, the man bears the burdens of humanity. Yet the history of the patriarchal church shows just the opposite: women have been impoverished, victims of domestic violence, forced into prostitution and raped both in war and in peace.

In 1984, Edwina Sandys unveiled Christa at the Cathedral of St. John the Divine in New York's Upper West Side. A haunting sculpture of a woman crucified, Christa is one of the most **significant works of art** created in modern times. There is nothing like it in history, yet history is littered with what it portrays. It took 2,000 years for a female artist to finally sculpt a naked woman on the cross, to finally announce to the world: Woman suffers, too. Woman bears the burdens of humanity, too.

The **Good News** is that bigotry and ignorance can persist but never prevail. Those religious groups that marginalize women marginalize themselves. They crucify themselves in the minds and hearts of good people of all faiths. "Spirit Crucified" symbolizes not the crucifixion but the crucifixion of crucifixion—the end of subordination and oppression and the

dawn of a new era

of egalitarianism. We may not be there in practice—yet—but now more than ever we are there in heart and in hope.

http://www.lostspiritualworld.com

Mark 16: 1-8

[1]And when the sabbath day was over, Mary of Magdala and Mary the mother of James and Salome bought spices so they could go and embalm him. [2]And very early on Sunday they got to the tomb just as the sun was coming up. [3]And they had been asking themselves, "Who will help us roll the stone away from the opening of the tomb?" [4]Then they look up and discover that the stone has been rolled away! (For in fact the stone was very large.) [5]And when they went into the tomb, they saw a young man sitting on the right, wearing a white robe, and they grew apprehensive. [6]He says to them, "Don't be alarmed! You are looking for Jesus the Nazarene who was crucified. He was raised, he is not here! Look at the spot where they put him! [7]But go and tell his disciples, including 'Rock,' 'He is going ahead of you to Galilee! There you will see him, just as he told you.'" [8]And once they got outside, they ran away from the tomb, because great

FEAR AND EXCITEMENT

got the better of them. And they didn't breathe a word of it to anyone: talk about

TERRIFIED...

2

EPILOGUE

Jesus was abandoned by everyone—his disciples, the pass-ersby, the Jewish scribes, the Roman soldiers. This is our worst fear: that we jump from the safety of the boat and slip into an unknown abyss whose promise may never be fulfilled. That Jesus bellowed a cry of abandonment, and that Mark shared with us this agonizing moment, trans-forms all that we have read until now. If Jesus knew all along that things would work out grandly in the end, then he merely felt a few hours of physical pain. But in his dying breath he suffered the cruelest form of abandonment, the painful realization that maybe his life was in vain and that maybe he was not the man he thought he was. Jesus' terrible final shout was for us: "I, too, have suffered your **worst fear**. I, too, was abandoned."

Mark portrays a prophet not understood by his own family, his own people or his own disciples. He never quite makes sense of the crucifixion. His message resonated for numerous first century Christians of Rome, persecuted by Nero, but it is a tough sell for third millennium seekers. In the contro-versy of Jesus' crucifixion, we are reminded that Mark's is only one of four accounts and that we must suspend judg-ment until we read the other three. In later volumes of the Lost Spiritual World series, especially Luke, we will see how the crucifixion was transformed from a historical event into a profound meditation on **suffering** and **forgiveness**.

According to Mark, Jesus could not always perform miracles and could be angry and vindictive, at times; but he did not suffer and die in vain. As Bruce Chilton writes, "Jesus' force resides in his **vulnerability** not only on the cross but throughout his life. He entices each of us to meet him in that dangerous place where an awareness of our own weakness and fragility shatters the self and blossoms into

an image of God within us."

Suffering stirs us to **transcend our limitations** and find a deeper meaning in the void of disbelief. From Jesus' suffering grew a mighty church. But the rock of the church is not built upon a literal belief in his bodily resurrection. Mark's ending is by far the best, for it is a cliffhanger and contains no embellishment about the supposed ascension of Jesus' physical body into Heaven. Of all the doctrines, this drives away third millennium seekers in droves. It is beautifully, joyfully absent from Mark, whose Gospel is the first and likely most accurate. The beauty of Mark's ending is that it has no ending.

The women were terrified because they came to the sudden realization that Jesus had tapped into **a new kind of Spiritual Power.** At that moment of fear and recognition, the Cosmic Christ was "risen" inside their hearts. They were the first to encounter the Cosmic Christ that we now encounter—not the historical Jesus of the body but the eternal Cosmic Christ of the Spirit. At that moment, they jumped into the Sea.

A literal, black and white worldview blinds us to the lost truths that the early Jewish and Christian writers could only hint at through metaphor. To experience the resurrection is to experience an **awakening**, a summons to embark upon an indescribably beautiful spiritual journey. You live again, you are freed from the shackles of your past, because you are flooded with the love that a billion souls since have felt burning hot within their hearts.

Jesus died on a Friday and his resurrection happened on a Monday, the beginning of the work week. Your soul needs work, too, and today will be

a New Monday
inside your heart.

Just as Jesus asked Peter, "Who do you say I am?" the Cosmic Christ asks you, "What do you say the end of this Gospel really means?" Mark provided no answer, not even a clue; for he realized that the question must be freshly asked and freshly answered by each generation. At the dawn of the third millennium, we find ourselves still swimming alongside Salome and the two Marys—still searching, still afraid, but never too afraid to leap into God's Sea.

http://www.lostspiritualworld.com/friends.html

RUTH RIMM

http://www.lostspiritualworld.com/friends.html

THE
LOST
SPIRITUAL
WORLD
FRIENDS
OF RUTH
CLUB

The mission of the *Lost Spiritual World*™ series is to foster an environment of peace, love, empathy, forgiveness, tolerance, pluralism, inclusivity and reconciliation through beautiful artwork, inspiring commentary and fresh translations of the Scriptures of our great wisdom traditions. The series finds good in all traditions and, while acknowledging important differences, accepts none as superior.

If you share these values and this mission, we invite you to participate in the series' evolution. If you join our *Friends of Ruth Club*, you will have the opportunity to review a draft of each edition before it is published, offer comments and suggestions, and even see yourself quoted in the final work. You will also have exclusive opportunities to purchase advanced and limited, autographed first editions.

A book can't change the world, but the people who come together to discuss and share a book most definitely can. The Dalai Lama said, "Be the peace that you wish to see in the world." We invite you to be the peace with us on this incredible journey.

For more information, please visit:
www.lostspiritualworld.com/friends.html

WWW.LOSTSPIRITUALWORLD.COM/FRIENDS.HTML

http://www.lostspiritualworld.com/gita.html

The Lost Spiritual World™ of the Bhagavad Gita helps you to discover *darsan*, the experience of seeing the world in a divine way. You will learn why seeing is a form of prayer, a mystical way of touching the sacred with your eyes. You will discover how blessings are given, wisdom is transmitted, and secrets are told — visually.

In the *Bhagavad Gita*, you will explore why intimacy with the Gods is visual. When Arjuna sees "the moon and the sun" in the eyes of Krishna, he sees a divine image and experiences darsan. Find out why the eyes, so often suspect in the West, are sacred in the Hindu tradition.

The Hindu Gods look nothing like anything you normally see on earth. They are fantastic, multifarious, with multiple arms, heads and colors. They stretch your imagination toward the divine by blending the mundane with the miraculous. This remarkable edition, rich in purple, pink and lavender metallic inks, helps you to see what you cannot easily see — or even imagine.

THE LOST SPIRITUAL WORLD™ OF THE BHAGAVAD GITA

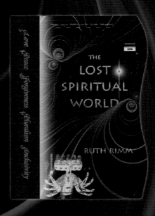

For a sneak preview, join the *Friends of Ruth Club.*
www.lostspiritualworld.com/friends.html

http://www.lostspiritualworld.com/buddha.html

THE
LOST
SPIRITUAL
WORLD™
OF THE
BUDDHA

Through breathtaking illustrations of the Sutras in gold and silver, Ruth Rimm takes you on a deep spiritual dive into the wisdom of the Buddha. Building on a tradition nearly two thousand years old, she shows why the Sanskrit characters are not mere arbitrary signs but have deep cosmic significance.

Ruth draws on recent findings in neuroscience to explain why the sight of a Buddhist image can trigger electrochemical responses in your brain. The images not only illuminate the text, they also open your mind and heart in brilliant new ways.

You will also gain a deeper appreciation of the spiritual nuance of color and how it applies to your everyday life. You will discover how many Eastern traditions used color to symbolize the various spiritual states of the Buddha.

By combining cutting-edge artwork with ancient topics such as the "Power of Faith," the "Perfection of Charity" and "Absolute Nothingness," *The Lost Spiritual World™ of the Buddha* takes you on an unforgettable spiritual journey.

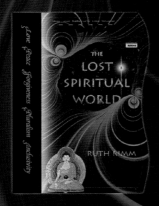

For a sneak preview, join the *Friends of Ruth Club.*
www.lostspiritualworld.com/friends.html

http://www.lostspiritualworld.com/sufi.html

In this rapturous marriage of calligraphy with gold, green and purple metallic inks, you will explore the long lost world of the Sufi mystics. Ruth Rimm takes you on a joyous exploration of the *'ilm al-qulub*, the "Science of the Hearts," through generous selections of Rumi, Rabia, Bayazid Bastami, and others.

Ruth honors the great tradition of Islamic illuminated manuscripts with stunning patterns, symmetries, and ecstatic combinations of form and color. The words wind and wave and ebb and flow about the page, while the fluffy white strokes make you feel as though you are "floating in the clouds." Many pages are coated in gold, in what the Islamic calligraphers called "the golden ecstasy."

Often called the "mystical branch" of Islam, Sufism originates in the teachings of the Prophet Muhammad. The Sufi mystics believed that God seeks to manifest beauty by infusing himself into the natural world. *The Lost Spiritual World™ of the Sufi Mystics* will delight your eyes, warm your heart, and give you a unique experience of the beauty of God.

THE
LOST
SPIRITUAL
WORLD™
OF THE
SUFI
MYSTICS

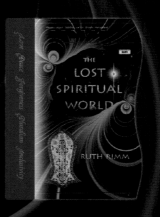

For a sneak preview, join the *Friends of Ruth Club*.
www.lostspiritualworld.com/friends.html

http://www.lostspiritualworld.com/luke.html

THE
LOST
SPIRITUAL
WORLD™
OF
LUKE

The Lost Spiritual World™ of Luke expands on many of the groundbreaking motifs first presented in Mark. You will experience stunning visual renditions of the three great hymns of the Church – the *Magnificat*, the *Benedictus* and the *Nunc Dimittis*, with the text of the *Scholars Version* set joyously to a "visual musical" score.

Ruth adapts the most famous scenes in Luke to our times, showing, for example, a Muslim gently nurturing a wounded Jew left to rot along the roadside in the *Parable of the Good Samaritan*. She shows how Jesus could not possibly have been born of a virgin, but how the "virgin birth" metaphor has deep resonance for our times.

Of all the books in our great wisdom traditions, Luke offers the most profound meditation on empathy, forgiveness, and love of neighbor. Luke traces the descent of Jesus not to Abraham but to Adam, showing how we are all brothers and sisters, regardless of culture or creed. His Gospel screams pluralism, tolerance and inclusivity to a world that desperately needs to hear such words of love.

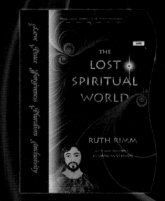

For a sneak preview, join the *Friends of Ruth Club*.
www.lostspiritualworld.com/friends.html

http://www.lostspiritualworld.com/moses.html

Will science, as Keats once feared, "conquer all mysteries, empty the haunted air, and unweave the rainbow"? Is Francis Crick correct? Are your joys and sorrows nothing more than "the behavior of a vast assembly of nerve cells and molecules?" If we know the mind of God, as Stephen Hawking once said, will we know everything on the mind of man? Is the dawn of our new complex civilization the death of privacy? Are private thoughts even possible? Is there any possibility of escape?

The Lost Spiritual World™ of Moses is a bold interpretation of the *Book of Exodus* for post-modern times. It is a profound meditation on privacy and freedom in a digital age in which all of our information is part of a vast public network.

Through a fresh examination of religious rituals and traditions, Ruth Rimm explores what may be the soul's last preserve of privacy and freedom. She dives deep into the laws of Moses, unearthing an unusual cache of spiritual treasures and adapting them to our times.

THE
LOST
SPIRITUAL
WORLD™
OF
MOSES

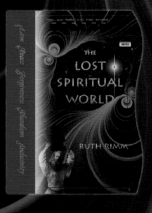

For a sneak preview, join the *Friends of Ruth Club*.
www.lostspiritualworld.com/friends.html

http://www.lostspiritualworld.com/whitman.html

THE
LOST
SPIRITUAL
WORLD™
OF
WHITMAN

Lo, soul! seest thou not God's purpose from the first?
The earth to be spann'd, connected by network,
The people to become brothers and sisters,
The races, neighbors, to marry and be given in marriage,
The oceans to be cross'd, the distant brought near,
The lands to be welded together.

In these remarkably prescient lines, written in 1872, Walt Whitman predicts our networked, pluralistic age. Though not a founder of a "religion" in any formal sense, Whitman wrote poetry as deep and as wise as any found in the Bible. Once the bard of the American frontier, he is now the bard of a new frontier, a new marriage of science and spirituality.

In *the Lost Spiritual World™ of Whitman*, Ruth Rimm pays homage to her favorite poet with rapturous commentary, earth-colored illustrations, and a lush symphony of green metallic inks. The mood of this handsome volume was best described by Whitman himself,

O we can wait no longer!
We too take ship, O soul!
Joyous, we too launch out on trackless seas!
Fearless, for unknown shores, on waves of ecstasy to sail.

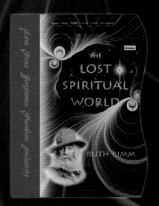

For a sneak preview, join the *Friends of Ruth Club*.
www.lostspiritualworld.com/friends.html

Journey http://www.goodbyegutenberg.com

EXPERIENCE THE RENAISSANCE.

How did an obscure high school English teacher in the Bronx, a young woman with no formal training as an artist, suddenly create the *Lost Spiritual World*™ series? How can you, likewise, tap into your deep well of creativity? How can you expand and transform your ability to communicate and impact the world?

Goodbye Gutenberg, Ruth Rimm's first book (written under her maiden name, Valerie Ruth Kirschenbaum), takes you on a mind-boggling, unforgettable journey into the future of reading and writing. In warm and intimate prose, Ruth shows you how and why we will experience a Renaissance of beautifully designed books in our lifetimes – and how you can be a part of it.

With 860 stunning, full-color images from the great manuscript traditions of the world, including Buddhist, Hindu, Chinese, Jewish, Christian, Muslim and Mayan, *Goodbye Gutenberg* provides the blueprint for an extraordinary new marriage of the verbal and visual arts. No verbal description can adequately describe the adventure you will take with this magnificent book. Order from your local bookstore or visit http://www.goodbyegutenberg.com.

Goodbye Gutenberg, pages 60-61.
Spread size is 9.3 x 16 inches

http://www.goodbyegutenberg.com

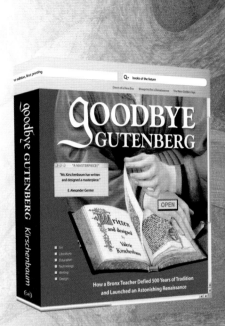

"Spectacular... dares Americans to read and dream by demonstrating the importance of colorful words in the literal sense... Highly recommended."
American Library Association's *Choice Magazine*

"Gorgeous and stimulating."
School Library Journal

"A remarkable and ground-breaking book."
Artvoice Magazine

"Probably one of the most stunningly visual books we've seen in the Design Bookshelf in some years. There's really nothing to compare. We would call it a visual masterpiece."
Design, Type & Graphics Magazine

"This book will unquestionably prove to be the inauguration of future debates pertaining to "designer writing" and the next era of the publication of fiction and non-fiction works of literature."
Bookpleasures' "Book of the Month" selection

"Bursting with information and ideas!"
Milton Glaser, world-renowned graphic artist

"Brilliant, beautiful and revolutionary!"
Martha Barletta,
CEO of Trendsights and author of *Marketing to Women*

"The ultimate showcase of what is now possible."
Dan Poynter, publishing expert

WINNER, ONE OF THE TEN MOST OUTSTANDING BOOKS OF 2004, INDEPENDENT PUBLISHERS BOOK AWARDS

WINNER, "BEST IN GRAPHIC DESIGN AND PUBLISHING" FOR 2004, DESIGN, TYPE & GRAPHICS MAGAZINE

WWW.GOODBYEGUTENBERG.COM

BOOK DESIGN http://www.lostspiritualworld.com/design.html

"COME PIONEER WITH US."

ASK RUTH RIMM TO DESIGN YOUR NEXT BOOK FOR YOU.

OR ASK HER TO TEACH YOU HOW.

Imagine creating a book inspired by the *Lost Spiritual World*, but with your own unique shape, your own choice of special inks, your own spiritual wavelength. Imagine creating a signature style that beautifully expresses who you are and the message you bring to the world. Imagine being one of the pioneers of the new Renaissance in book design, maybe even making a lasting contribution to our culture.

To submit an application and request your private consultation, please visit: www.lostspiritualworld.com/design.html.

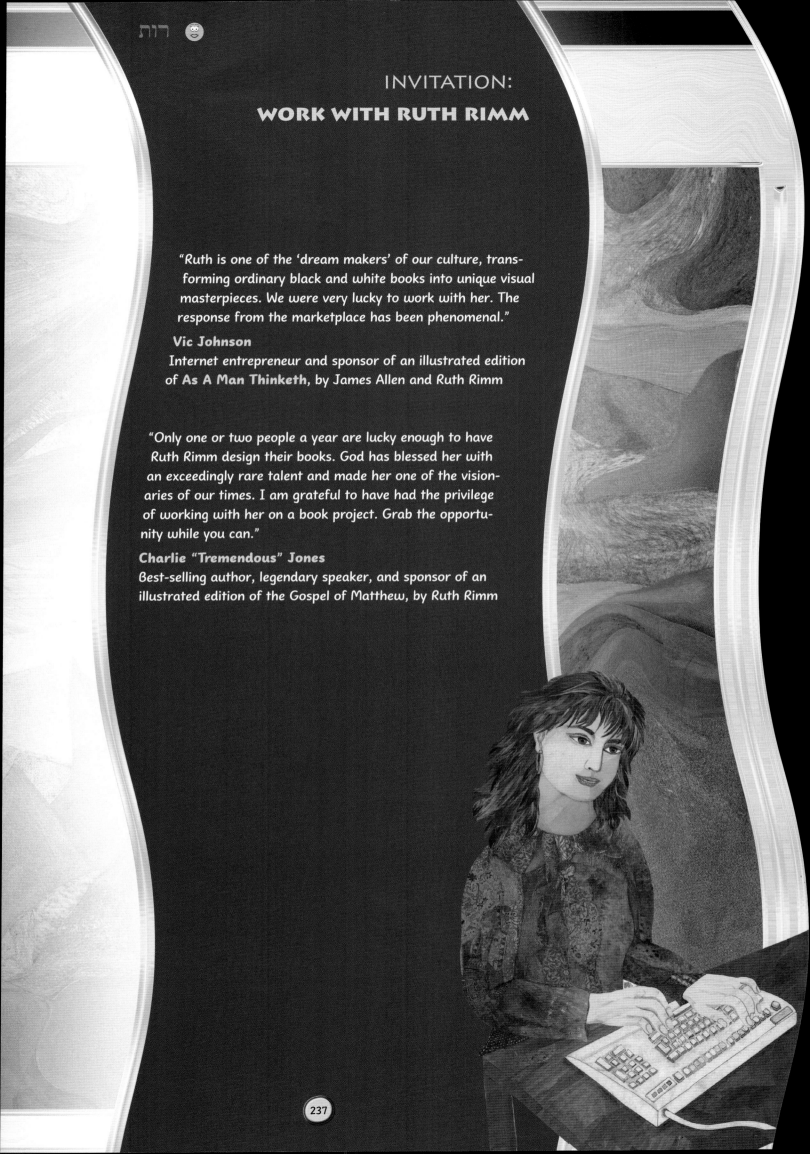

INVITATION:

WORK WITH RUTH RIMM

"Ruth is one of the 'dream makers' of our culture, transforming ordinary black and white books into unique visual masterpieces. We were very lucky to work with her. The response from the marketplace has been phenomenal."

Vic Johnson
Internet entrepreneur and sponsor of an illustrated edition of **As A Man Thinketh**, by James Allen and Ruth Rimm

"Only one or two people a year are lucky enough to have Ruth Rimm design their books. God has blessed her with an exceedingly rare talent and made her one of the visionaries of our times. I am grateful to have had the privilege of working with her on a book project. Grab the opportunity while you can."

Charlie "Tremendous" Jones
Best-selling author, legendary speaker, and sponsor of an illustrated edition of the Gospel of Matthew, by Ruth Rimm

Mark 16: 9-20 http://www.lostspiritualworld.com/ending.html

http://www.lostspiritualworld.com/ending.html ▼ **Mark 16: 9-20**

"THE VERSE THAT CHANGED HISTORY!"

MARK

THE SHOCKING ENDING

AN EBOOK

RUTH RIMM

I had so much help in the creation of this series that I hesitate to take credit and wish that at least a dozen other people could join my name on the title page. I am especially grateful to my husband and his remarkable circle of friends. I am more of the solitary creator type, whereas he excels at soliciting feedback and handling the thousand and one tasks (including late night trouble shooting, both technical and spiritual) necessary to complete a work as complex as this.

I extend my heartfelt gratitude to those who have blessed us along the way with their loving kindness and generous feedback and support. They include: Alejandra Vernon, (her self-portrait is below), Lydia Richards, Linda Crawford, Ian Percy, Scott Hines, Ian Clayton, Richard Shewman, John Assaraf, Murray Smith, Jim Hardt, Louis Cady, Bill Burdette, Michael Weiss, Eric Wood, Mary Rowles, Cynthia Murphy, Betty Rimm, Linda Bianchi, Bart Murray, Conrad Toner, Don Cramer, Aubrey Lynn, Joan Chittister, Erik Walker Wikstrom, Bruce Chilton, Charlie "Tremendous" Jones, Vic Johnson, Bob Proctor, B. Victor Williams, Greg Tucker, Tristram R. Fall, III, Rob Flank, Linda Getchell, Dr. Daniel J. Maloney, Steven Szmutko, Dan Holland, John Kremer, and the folks at CBC, a heartwarming evangelical Church that represents all that is good and noble about Christianity.

Ultimately, no matter the contributions of others, I finally realized that I must own up to this book. The heart and soul of it is mine, and that includes its shortcomings. It took me a long time to release myself from the need to make it perfect. I realize that in five years I will have a different spiritual perspective but that a later perspective is not necessarily better. It is simply different. We are all on a time continuum and the goal is to find peace in the moment, not perfection in eternity.

LOVE AND THANKS

ALEJANDRA VERNON

SELF PORTRAIT

MIDRASH:

PARABLE OF THE GOOD MUSLIM

Jesus originally told this parable to shock his listeners out of their prejudice, to open their hearts to the deeper truths of our common humanity. The Samaritans were a despised people, and the Jews were forbidden from having any contact with them. But Jesus said no; there are good-hearted people among the Samaritans, too.

It was a desperately needed parable at the time of Jesus and it is a desperately needed parable of our time, too. Only now, for so many in the West, the Samaritans are the Muslims, most of whom are good-hearted people, unfairly and unjustly ridiculed and despised.

This is the parable of the

Good Muslim.

A beaten Jew lies on the ground. He is stripped of his clothing, with the fringes of his garments soiled by the dirt. His fellow Jews and Christians went out of their way to avoid him. But here a devout Muslim nurtures him back to life, with a look of compassion on his face.

All too many Christians are denouncing Islam as a "religion of hate." Such venomous rhetoric leads only to more venom. In an age in which Western cartoonists are mocking Islam, and Islamic cartoonists, angered and hurt, retaliate by mocking the Holocaust and Christianity, we need imagery that exalts our neighbors, especially those of different faiths.

Excerpt from
The Lost Spiritual World of Luke
Coming Winter 2008